COMPLETE BOOK OF MONEY SAVINGS CHALLENGES

By C J Phillips

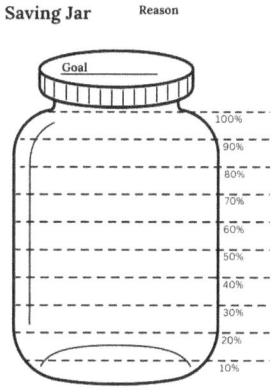

By purchasing this product you are supporting a small business and for that we thank you!

Scan the QR code below to connect with us on Amazon. By following us, you will receive the latest updates and new product releases, to help us on this incredible journey!

www.palette-of-possibilities.co.uk

COMPLETE BOOK OF MONEY SAVINGS CHALLENGES

By C J Phillips

ALL RIGHTS RESERVED
Unauthorised reproduction of any part of this book in any form or through any means, electronic or mechanical, including information storage and retrieval systems, is strictly prohibited without the written permission of the author.

TERMS OF USE:
This product is for PERSONAL USE ONLY
Files CANNOT be used commercially, or resold, or redistributed in any way.
Files are designed and developed by Service Awakenings Limited, company number 11004848 England & Wales
C J Phillips, Moneyandwealthqueen & Palette of Possibilities are all trading names of Service Awakenings Limited

Copyright © 2024 Service Awakenings LTD. All Rights Reserved

Save for.....
Timed Savings

Save $150 In 30 Days

Save $150
In 30 Days

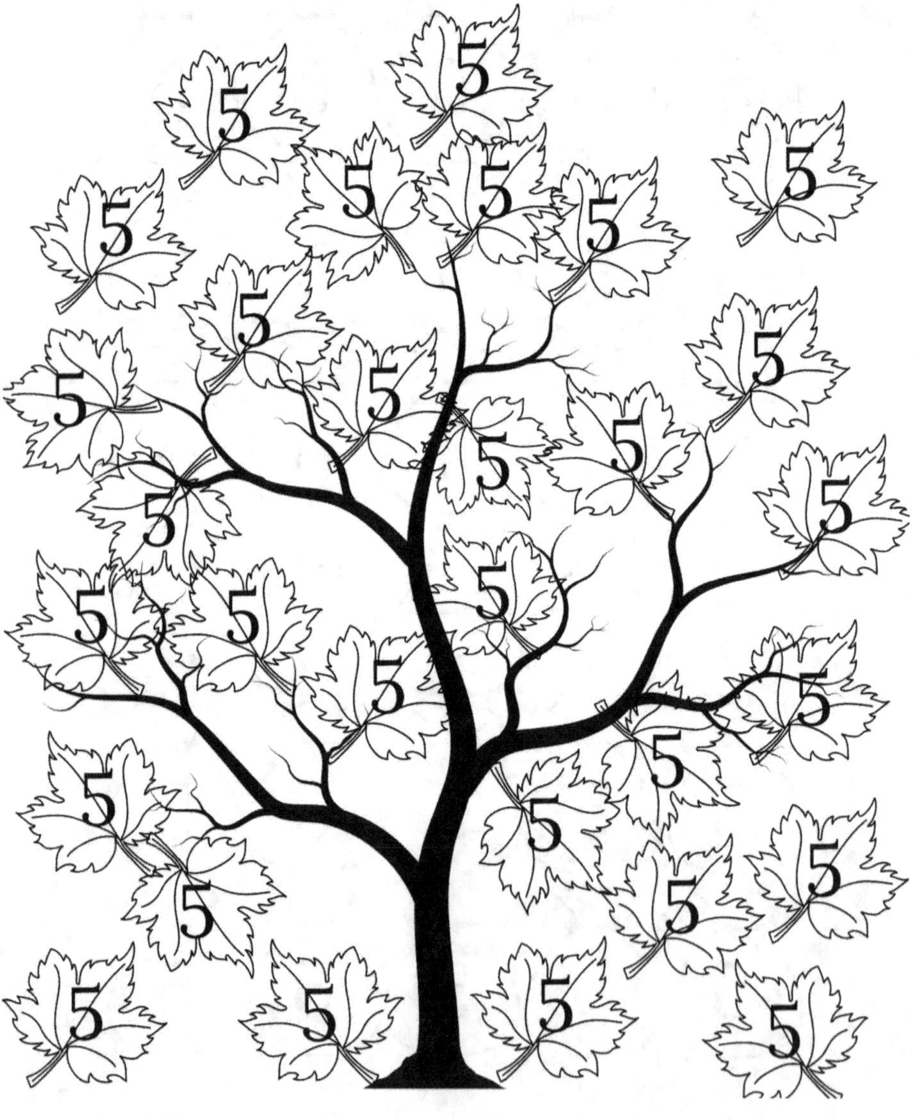

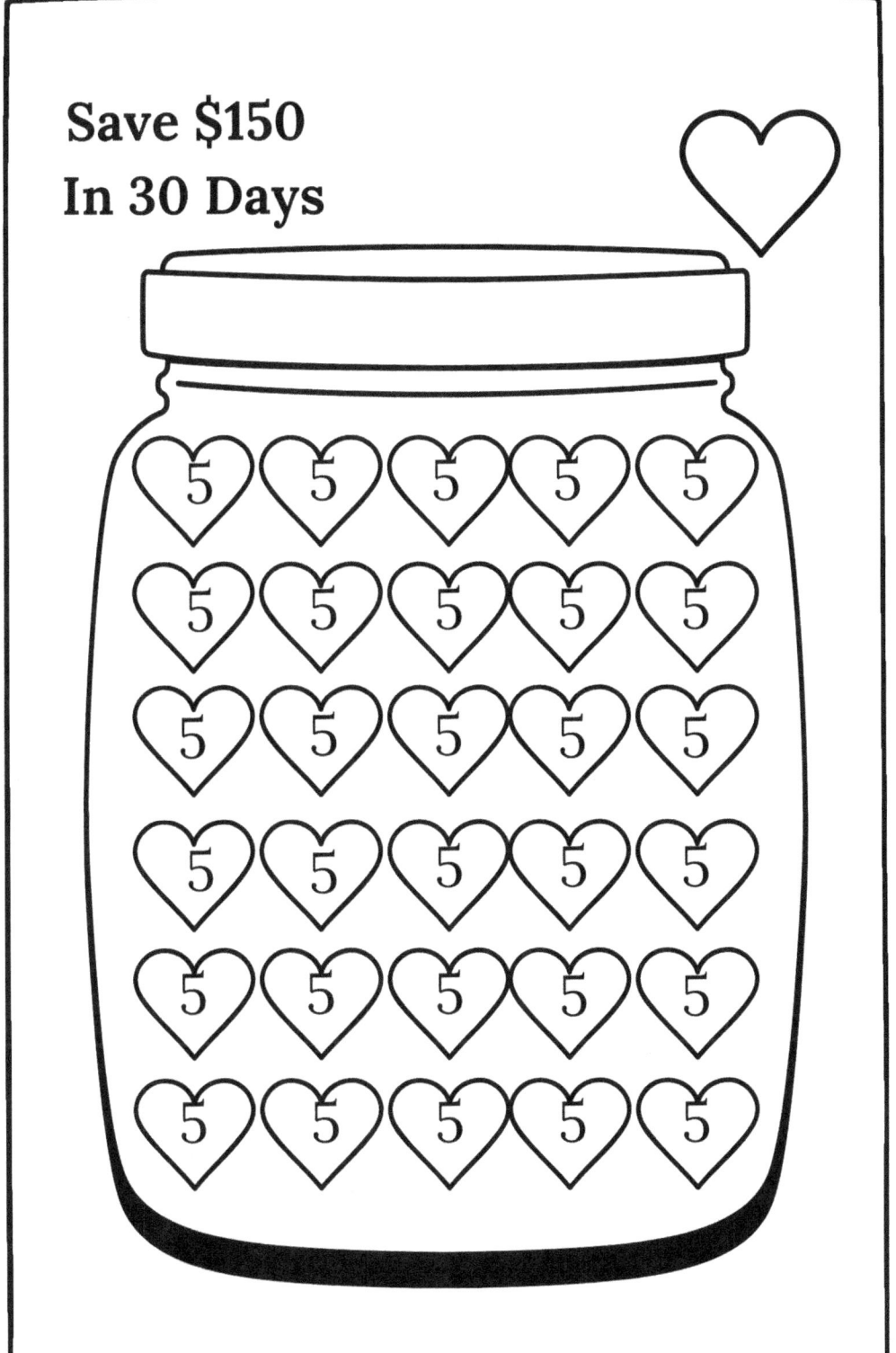

Save $150
In 30 Days

5	5	5	5	5
5	5	5	5	5
5	5	5	5	5
5	5	5	5	5
5	5	5	5	5
5	5	5	5	5

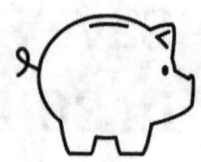

Save $300 In 30 Days

(10) (10) (10) (10) (10)
(10) (10) (10) (10) (10)
(10) (10) (10) (10) (10)
(10) (10) (10) (10) (10)
(10) (10) (10) (10) (10)
(10) (10) (10) (10) (10)

Save $300
In 30 Days

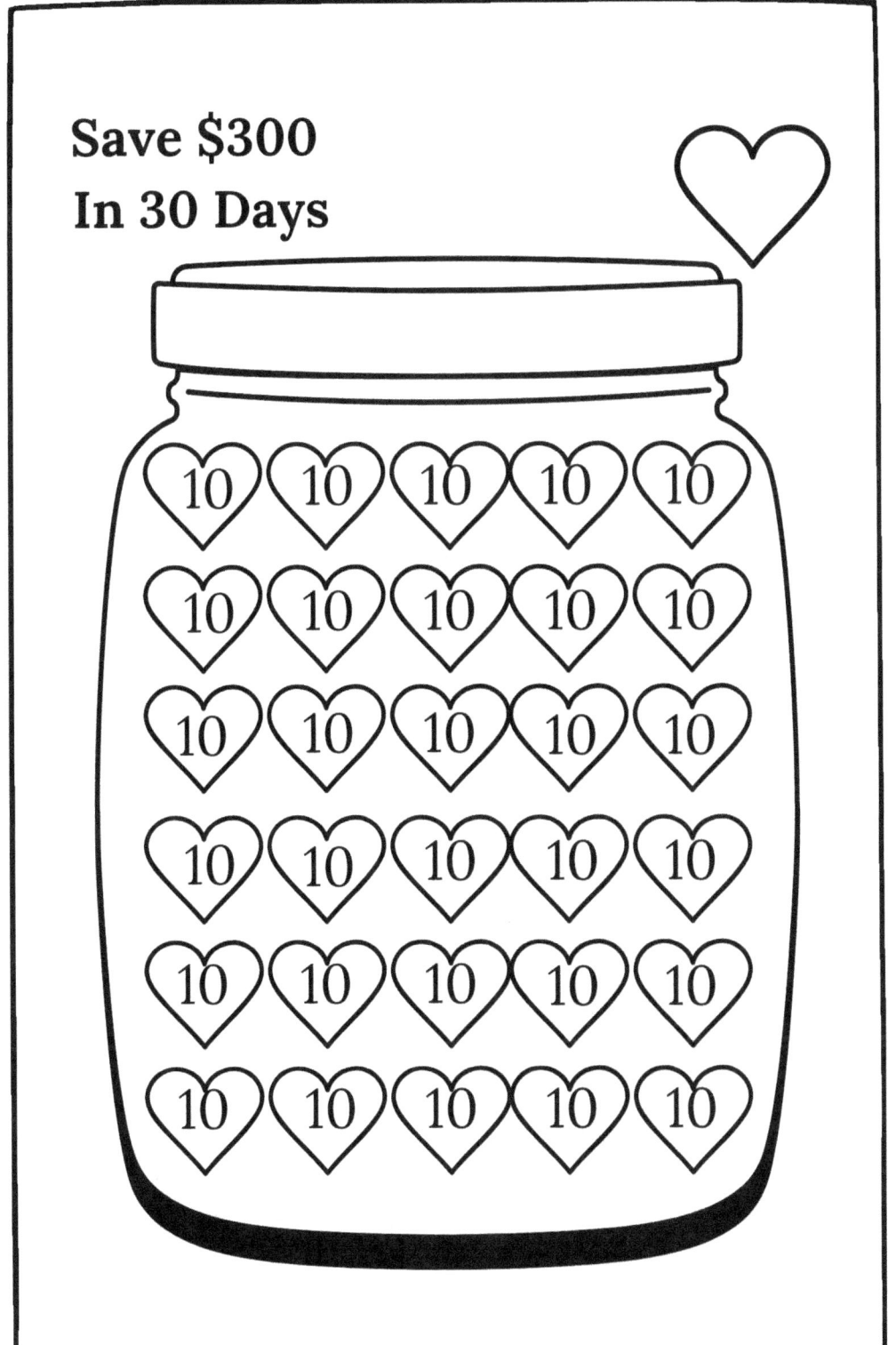

Save $300 In 30 Days

10 10 10 10 10

10 10 10 10 10

10 10 10 10 10

10 10 10 10 10

10 10 10 10 10

10 10 10 10 10

Save $500 In 30 Days

15	20	15	20	15
20	15	15	15	20
15	15	20	15	15
20	15	15	20	15
15	15	20	15	15
15	20	15	15	20

Save $500 In 30 Days

Save $500 In 30 Days

15	20	15	20	15
20	15	15	15	20
15	15	20	15	15
20	15	15	20	15
15	15	20	15	15
15	20	15	15	20

Save $500 In 30 Days

20	15	15	20	15
15	20	20	15	15
15	20	15	15	20
20	15	20	15	15
15	15	15	15	20
15	15	15	20	15

Save $1,000 In 30 Days

30	40	30	40	30
40	30	30	30	40
30	30	40	30	30
40	30	30	40	30
30	30	40	30	30
30	40	30	30	40

Save $1,000 In 30 Days

Save $1,000 In 30 Days

40	30	30	40	30
30	30	40	30	30
30	40	30	30	40
40	30	40	30	30
30	40	30	40	30
30	30	30	30	40

Save $1,000 In 30 Days

40	30	30	40	30
30	40	40	30	30
30	40	30	30	40
40	30	40	30	30
30	30	30	30	40
30	30	30	40	30

Save $1,200 in 12 Weeks

You Did It
100
100
100
100
100
100
100
100
100
100
100
100

Save $2,500 in 12 Weeks

	You Did It
	225
	200
	200
	225
	200
	200
	225
	200
	200
	200
	225
	200

Save $5,000 in 12 Weeks

You Did It
450
400
400
450
400
400
450
400
400
400
450
400

Save $7,500 in 12 Weeks

- You Did It
- 675
- 600
- 600
- 675
- 600
- 600
- 675
- 600
- 600
- 600
- 675
- 600

Let's Save $200 in 100 Days

Let's Save $500 in 100 Days

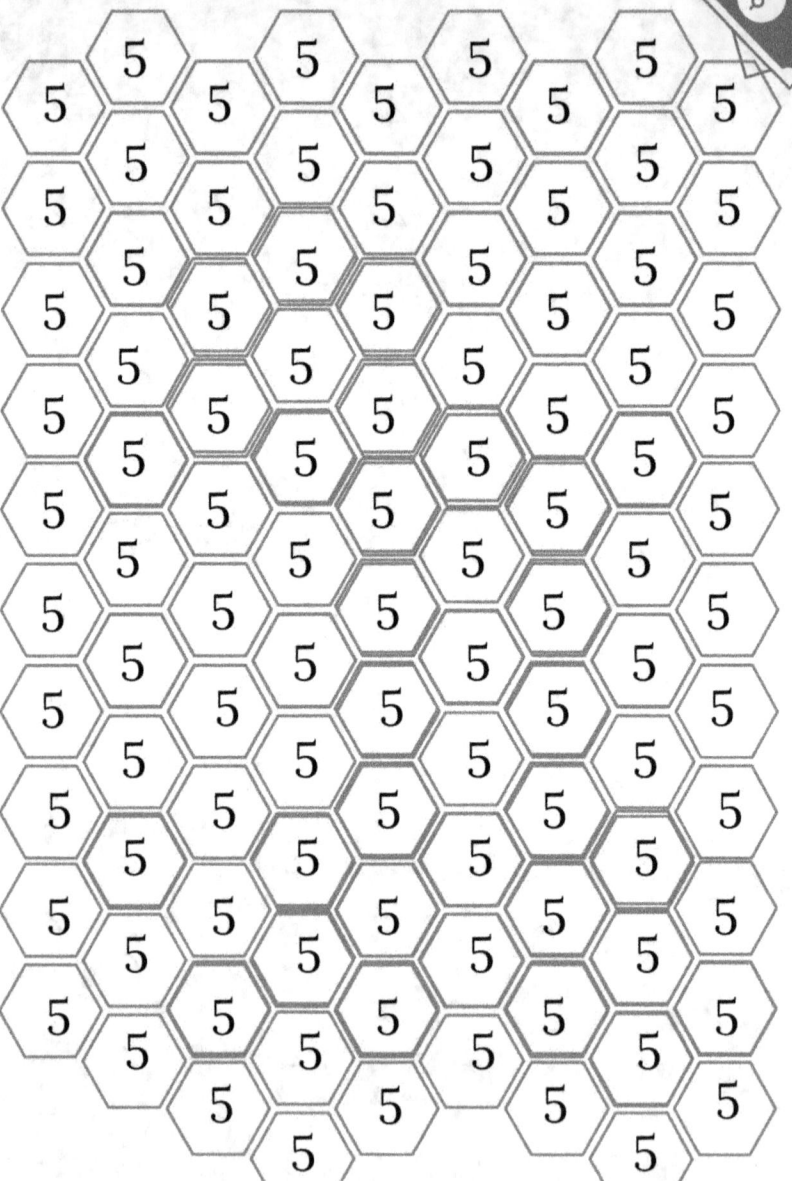

Let's Save $1,000 in 100 Days

Let's Save $2,000 in 100 Days

26 Weeks to Save $2,600

$100 Per Week

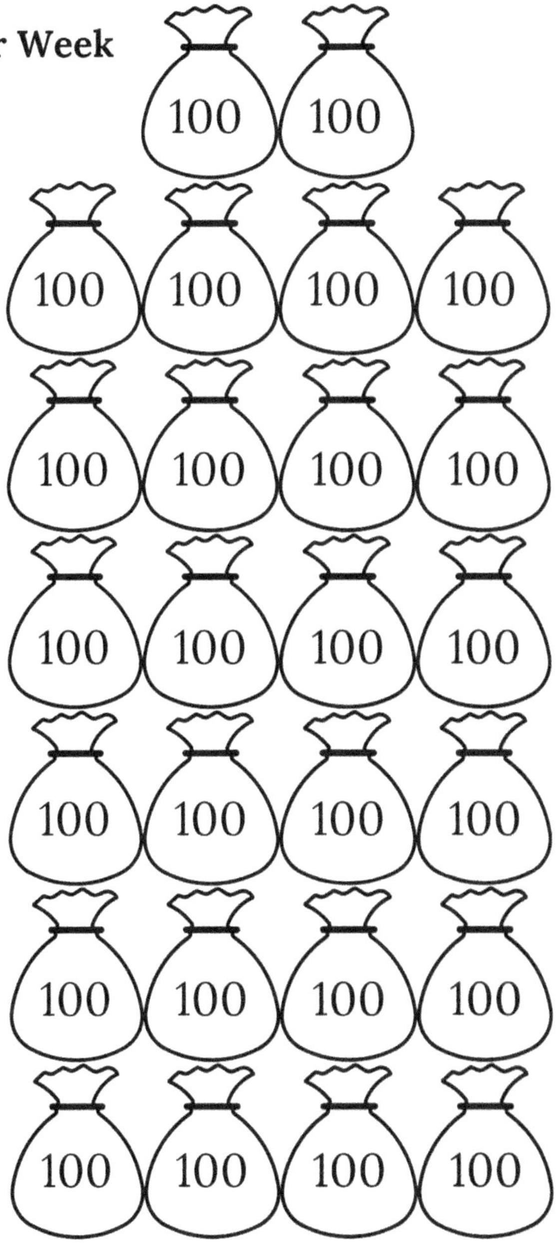

26 Weeks to Save $2,600

$100 Per Week

52 Weeks to Save $5,200

$100 Per Week

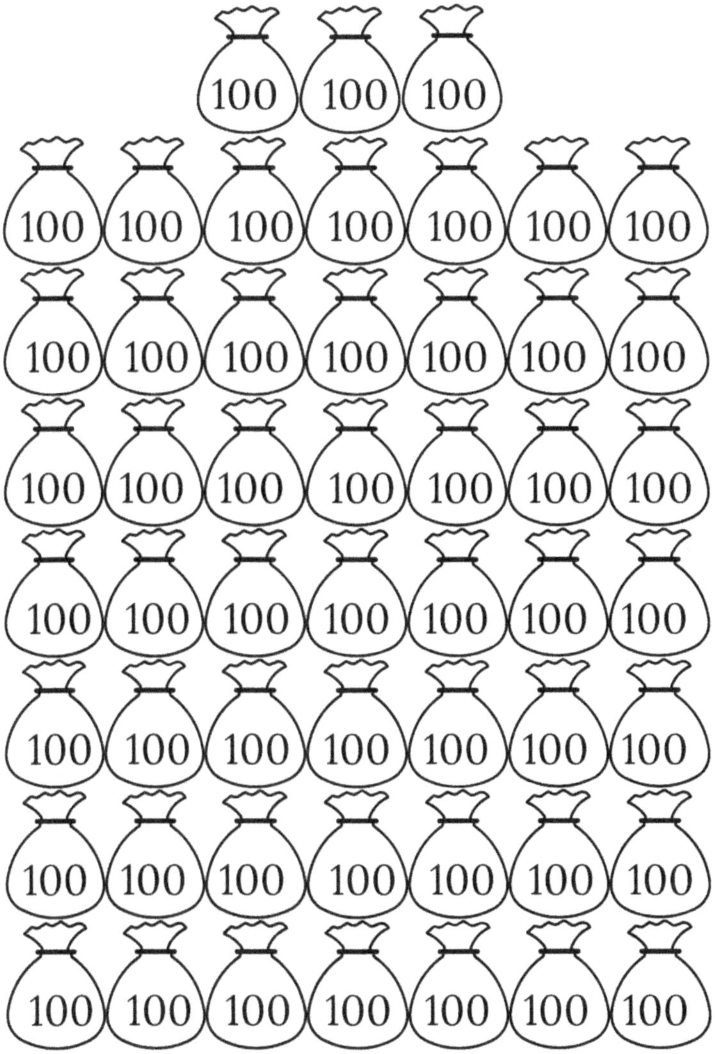

52 Weeks to Save $5,200

$100 Per Week

52 Weeks to Save $5,200
$100 per week

52 Weeks to Save $10,400

$200 Per Week

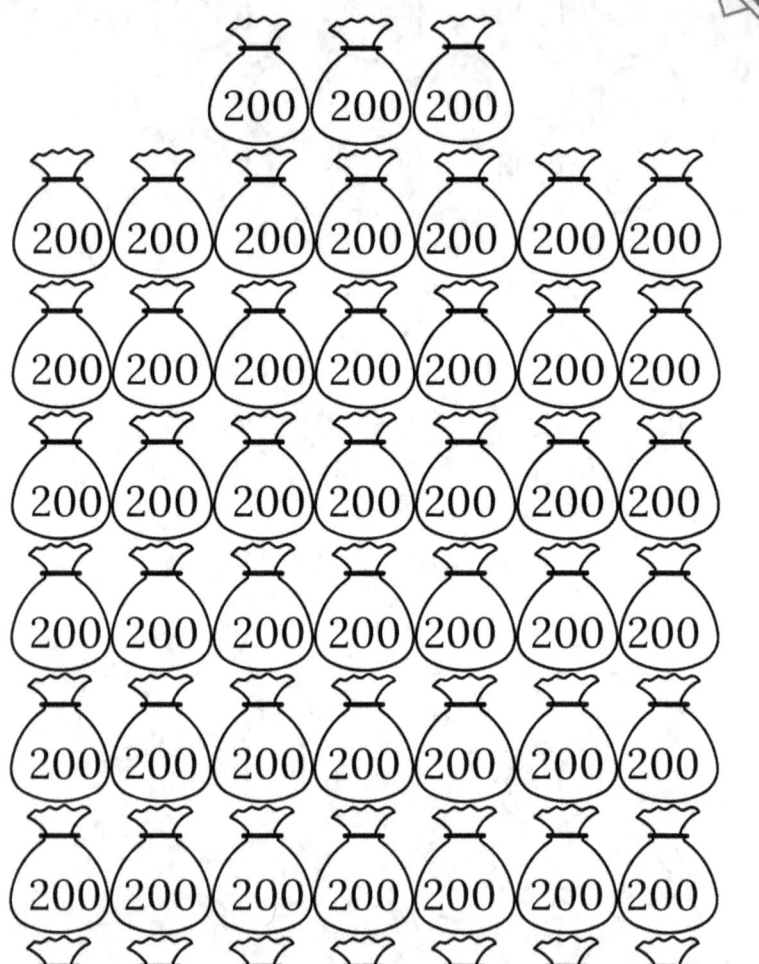

52 Weeks to Save $10,400

$200 Per Week

Save for.....
A Specific Amount

Turn $10 into $500 Savings

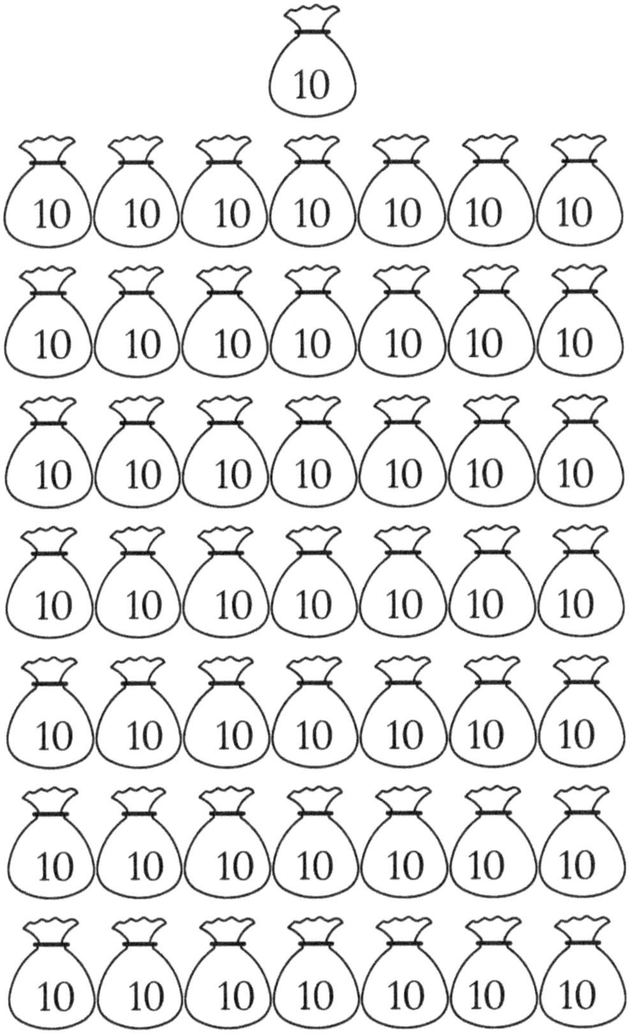

Turn $20 into $500 Savings

20	20	20	20	20
20	20	20	20	20
20	20	20	20	20
20	20	20	20	20
20	20	20	20	20

Turn $20 into $1,000 Savings

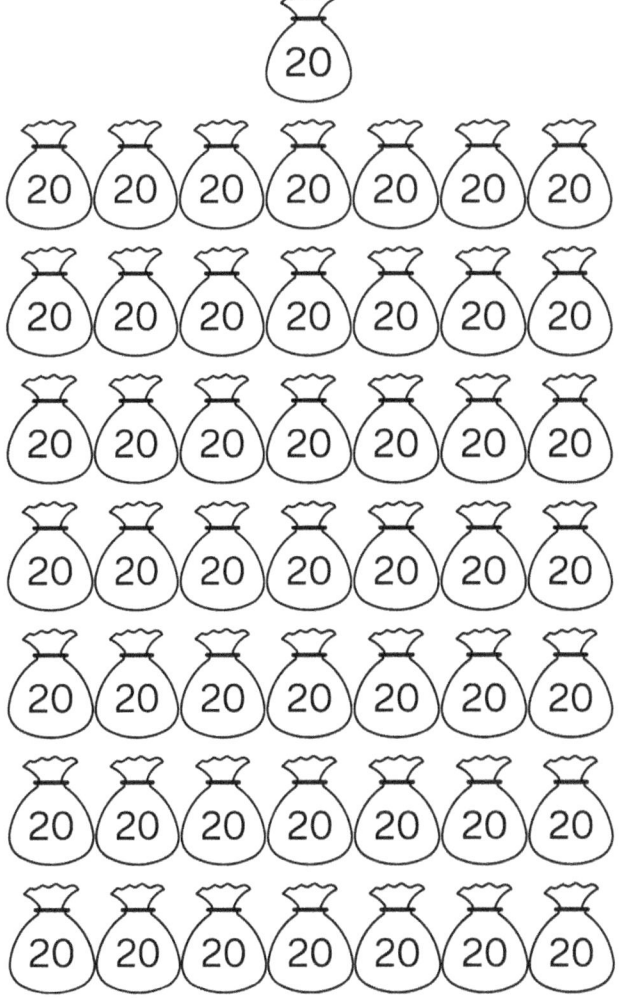

Turn $25 into $2,000 Savings

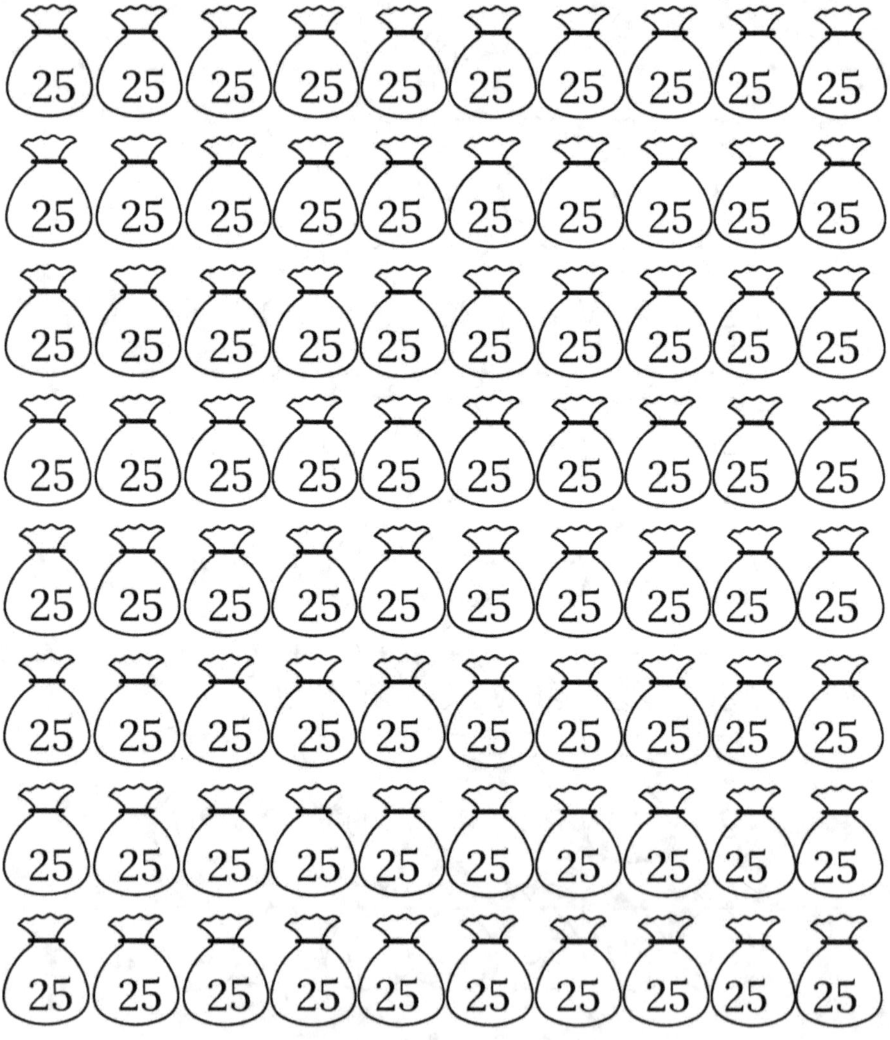

Let's Save $5,000

75	50	75	50	75	50	50	50	75	75
75	100	75	50	75	100	50	50	25	25
75	50	75	50	75	50	50	50	75	75
75	100	75	50	75	100	50	50	25	25
75	50	75	50	75	50	50	50	75	75
75	100	75	50	75	100	50	50	25	25
75	50	75	50	75	50	50	50	75	75
75	50	75	50	75	50	50	50	75	75

Let's Save $7,250

Let's Save $6,000

Save for.....

An Occasion

Holiday Savings Fund

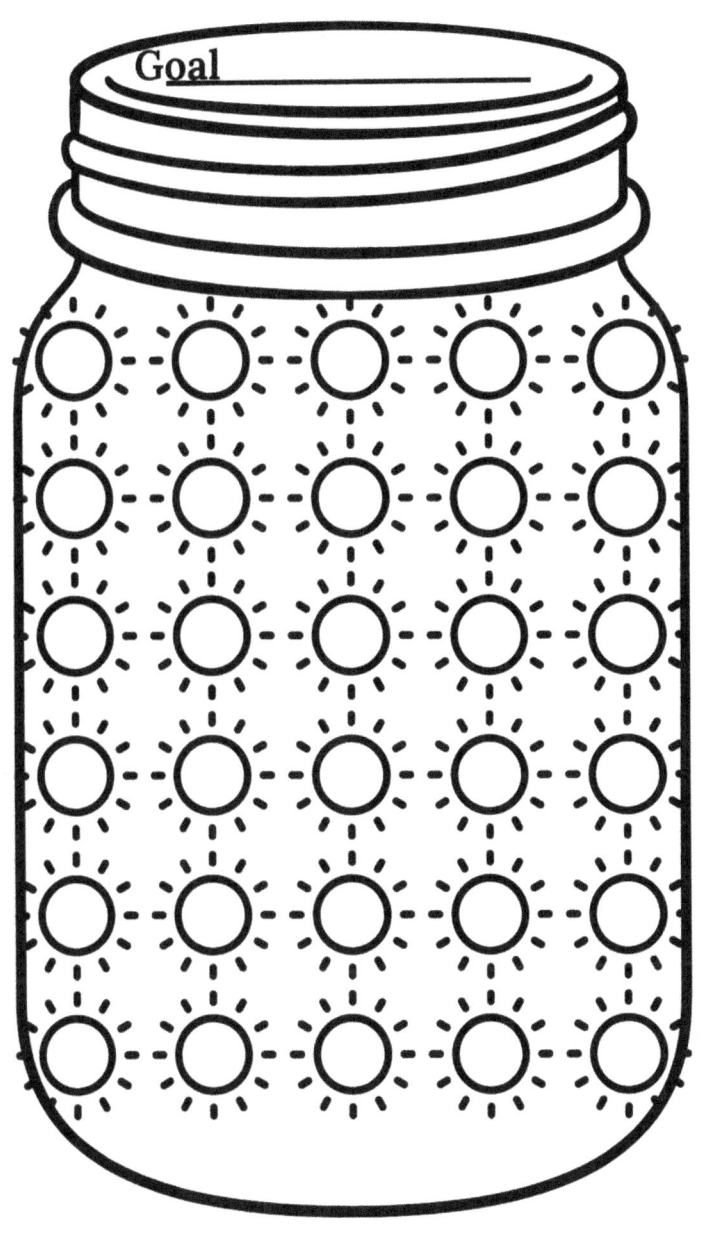

Vacation Fund

Goal _____

Vacation Fund

Goal _____

Vacation Fund

Goal _____

Vacation Fund

Goal _____

Vacation Fund

Goal _____

Weekend Away Fund

Goal _____

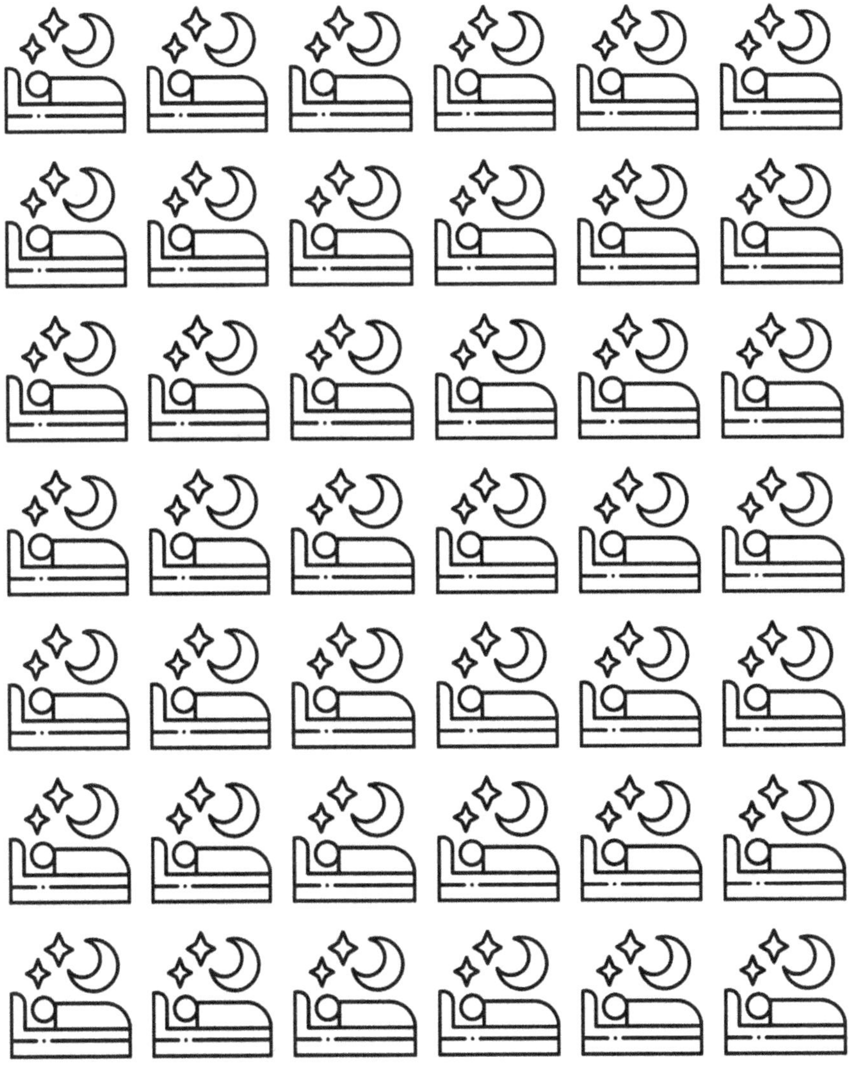

Weekend Away Fund

Goal _____

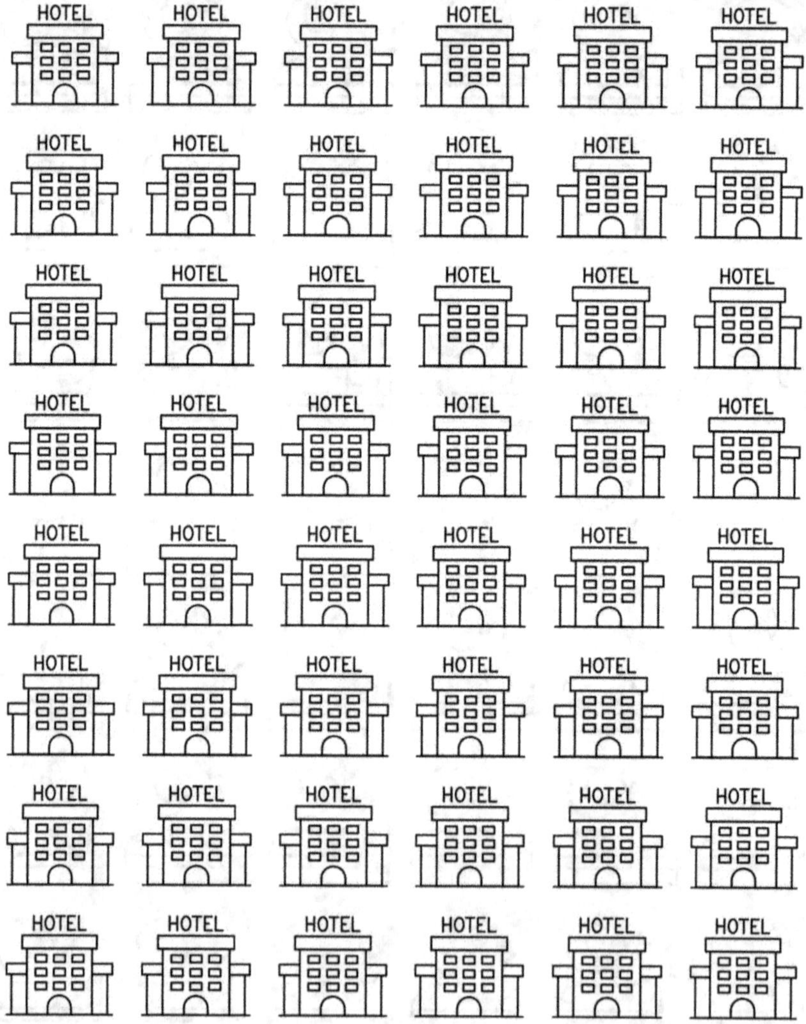

Weekend Away Fund

Goal _____

Birthday Saving Jar

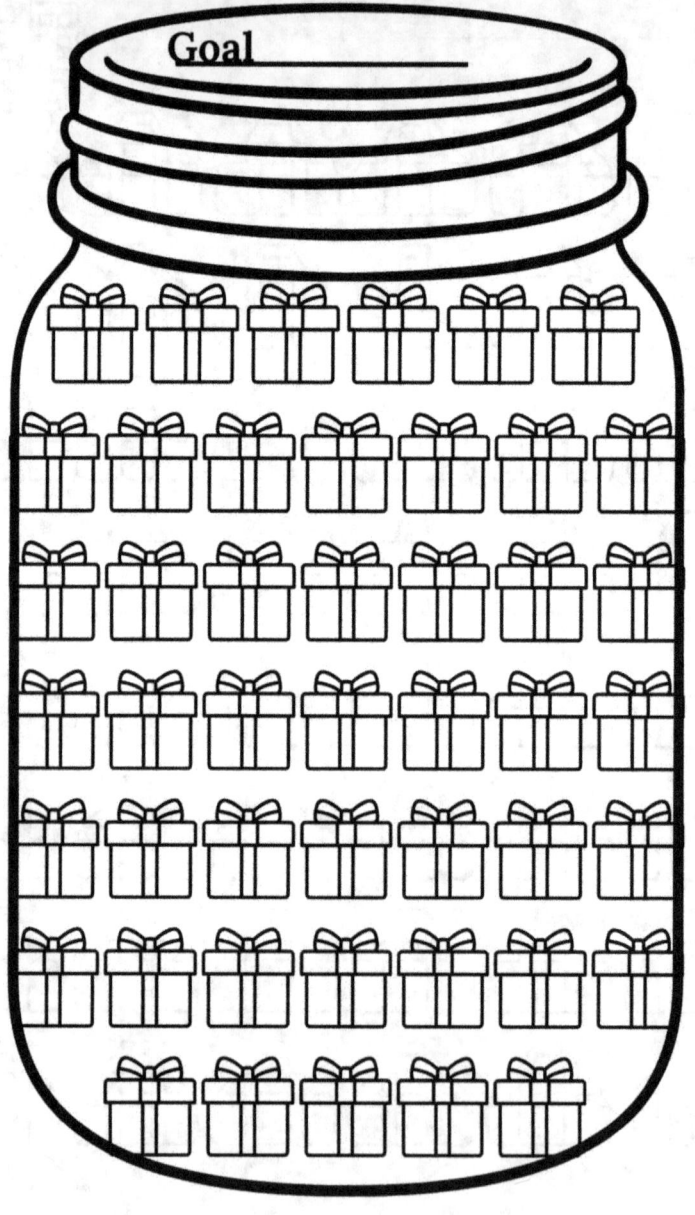

Birthday Saving Jar

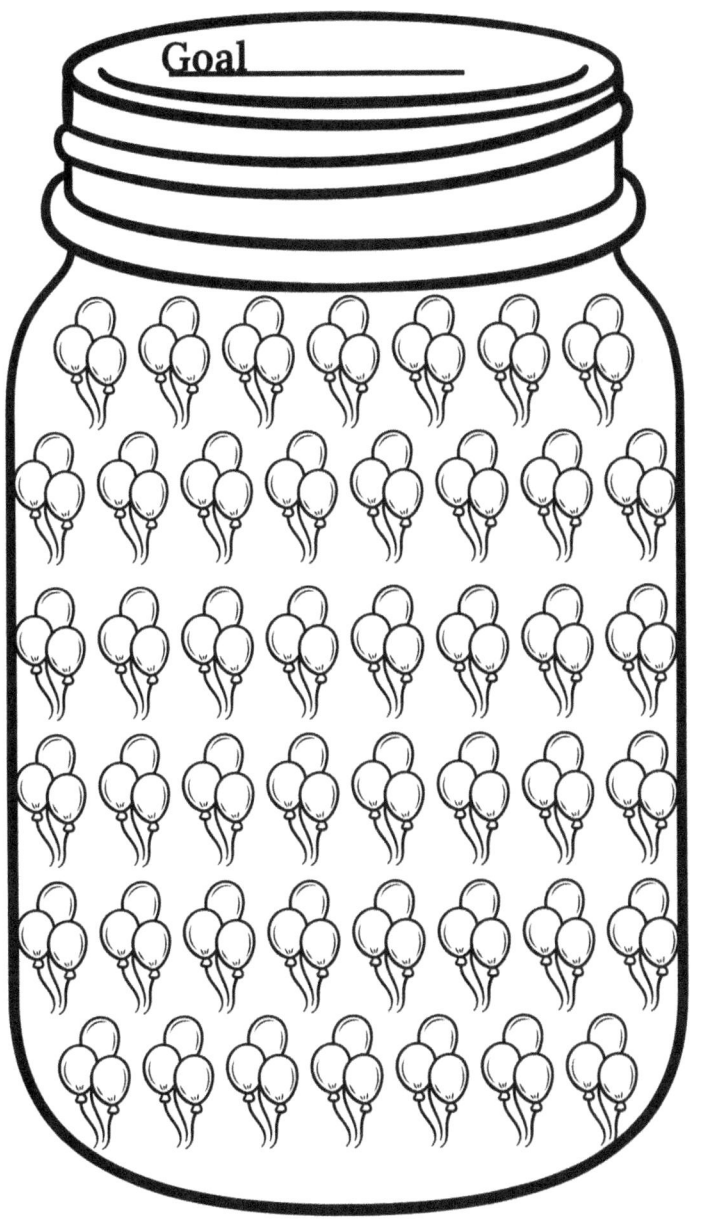

Goal _____

Birthday Saving Jar

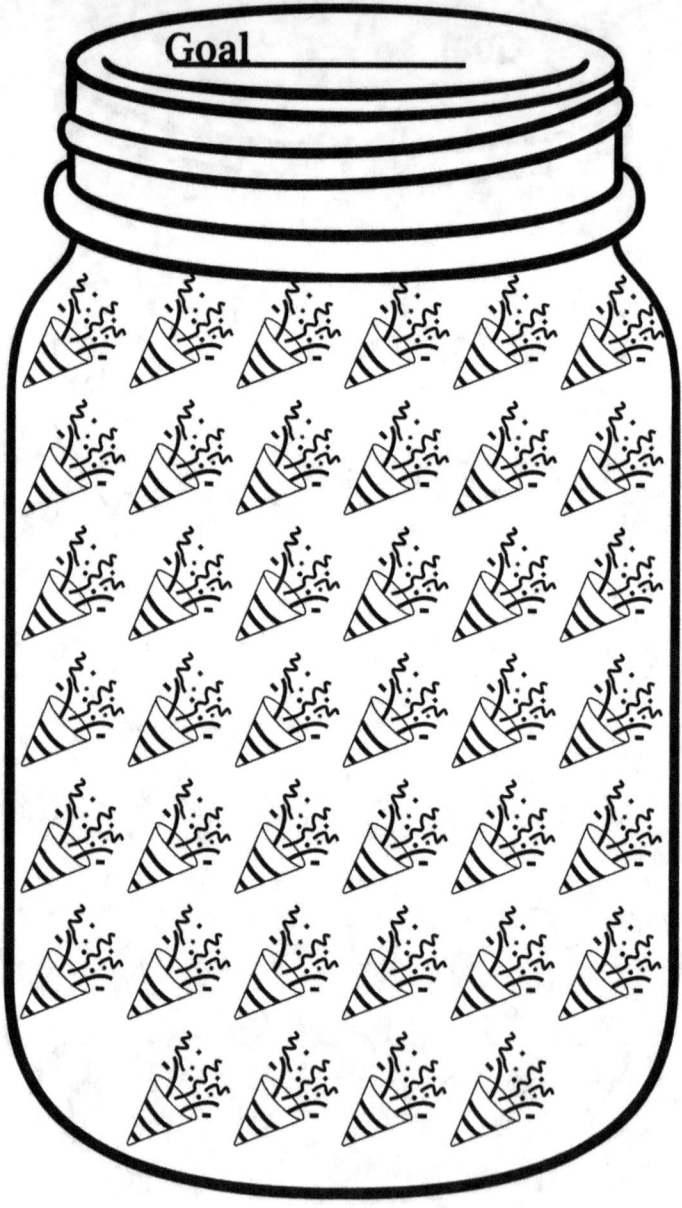

Goal _____

Birthday Saving Jar

Birthday Savings Fund

HAPPY Birthday

Goal ______________________________

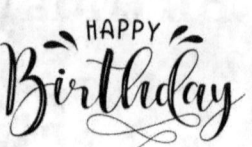

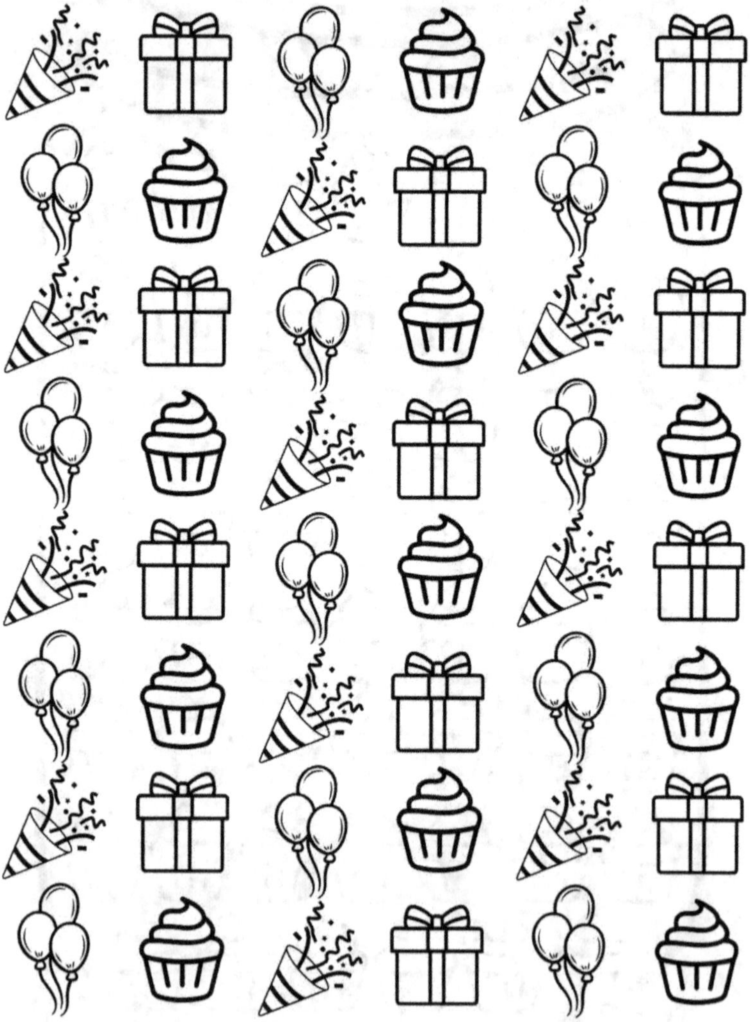

Toy Savings Fund

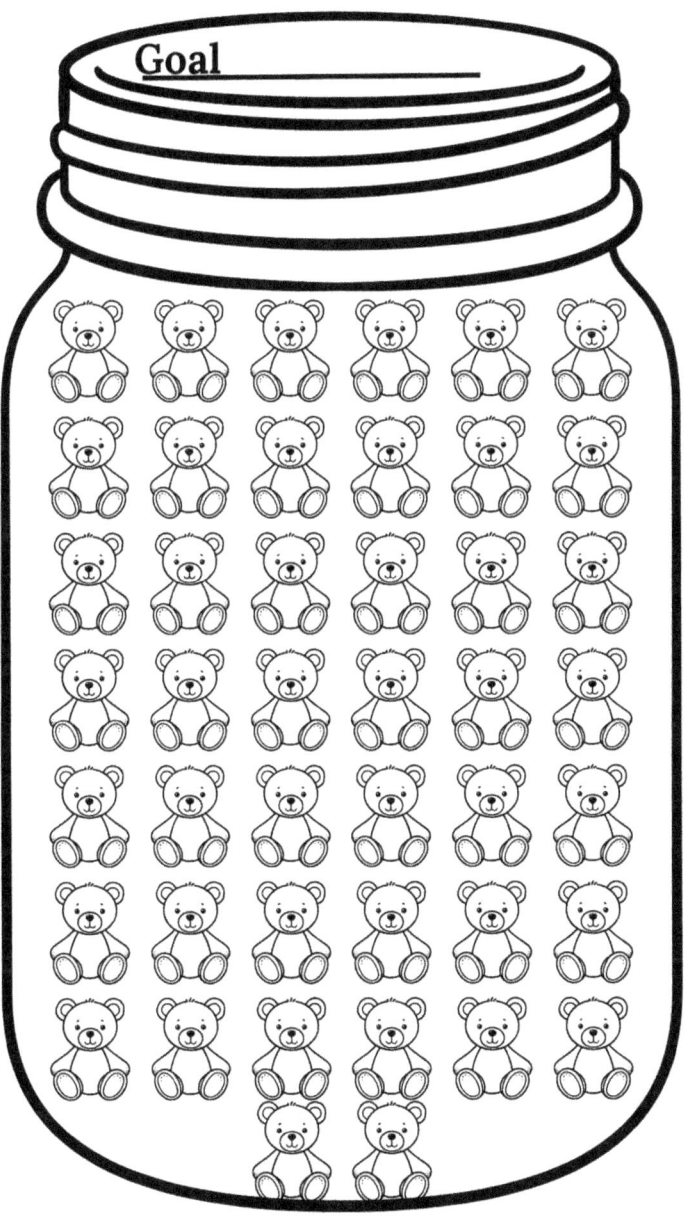

Goal _____

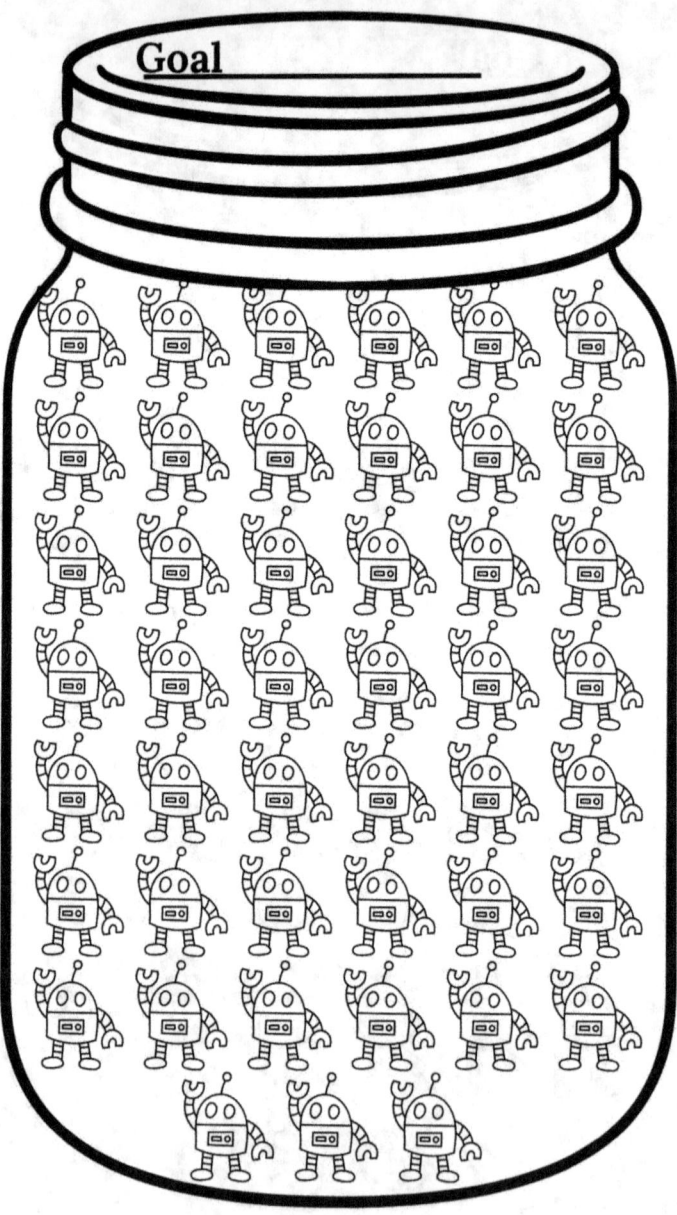

Toy Fund
Goal _____

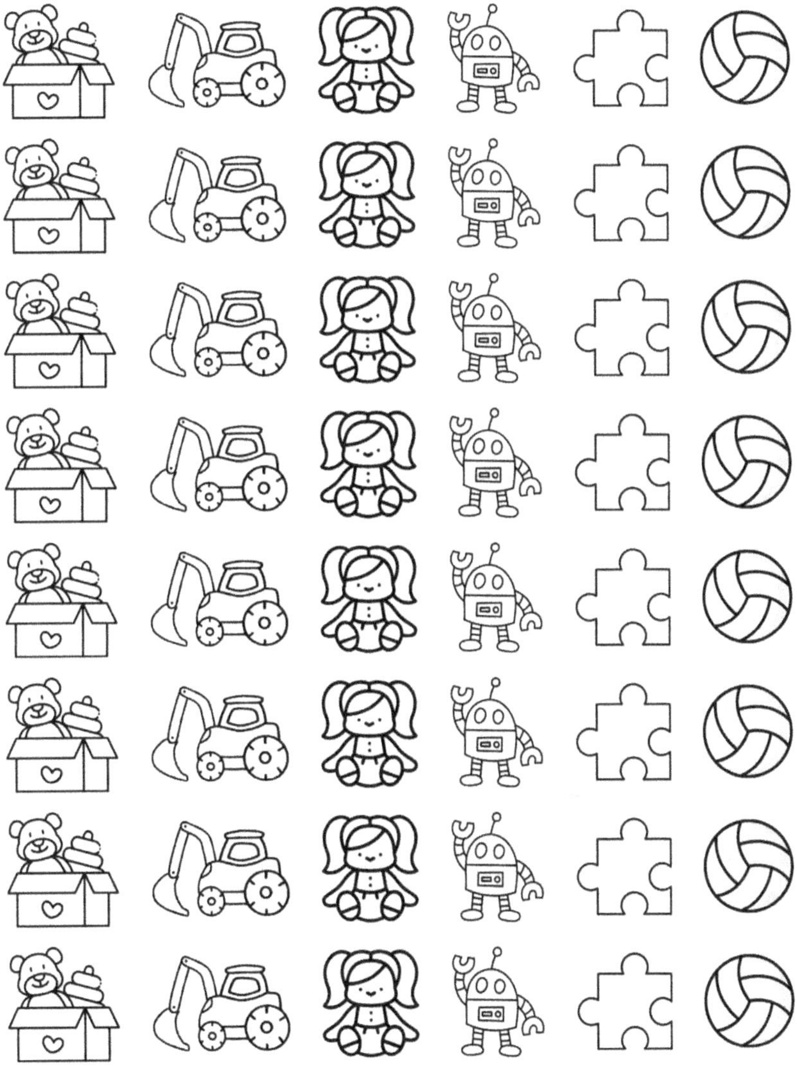

Wedding Fund

Goal _____

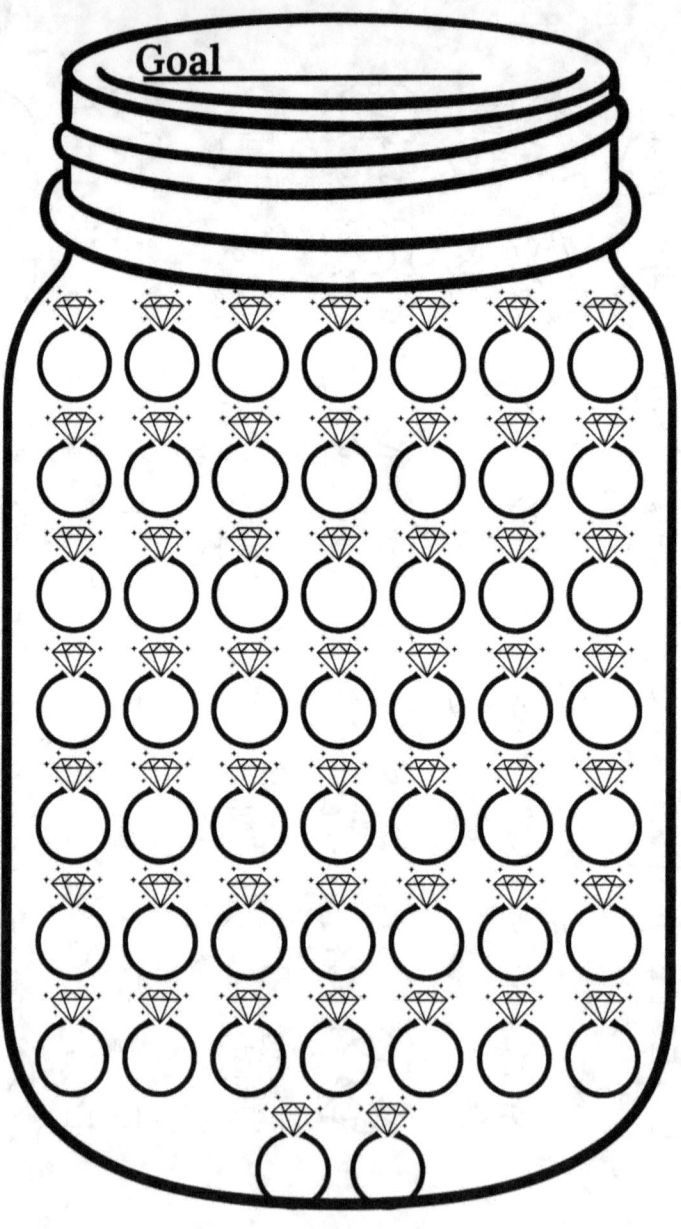

Wedding Dress Fund

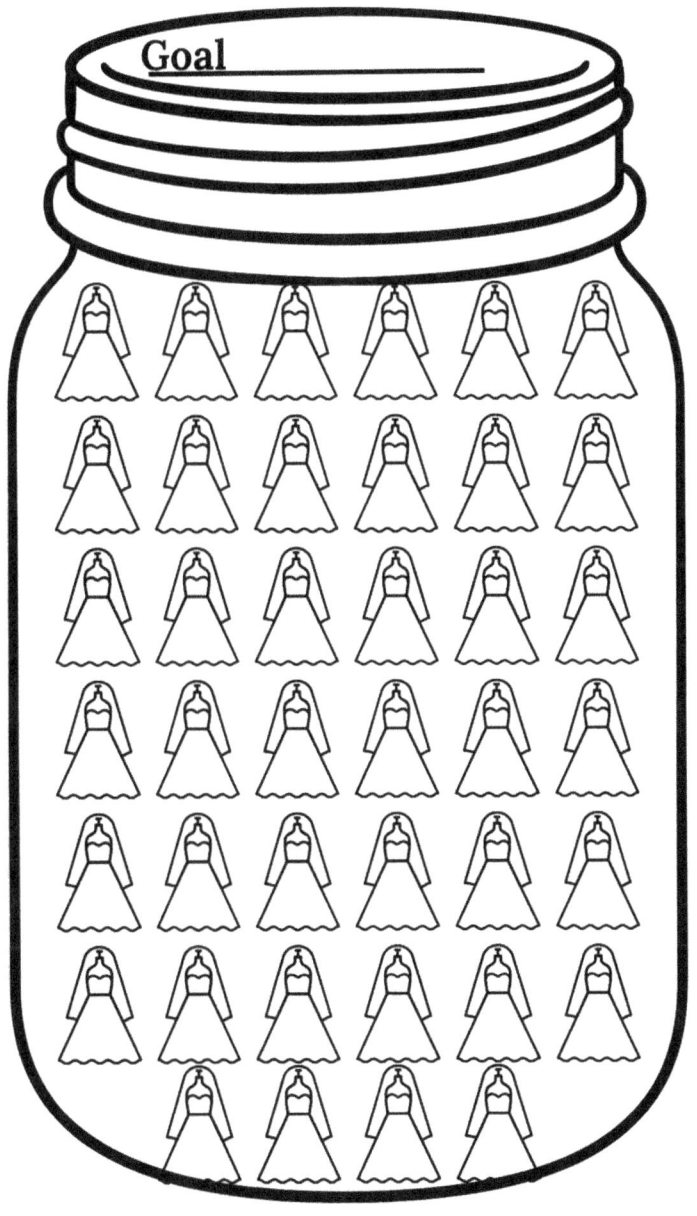

Wedding Fund

Goal _____

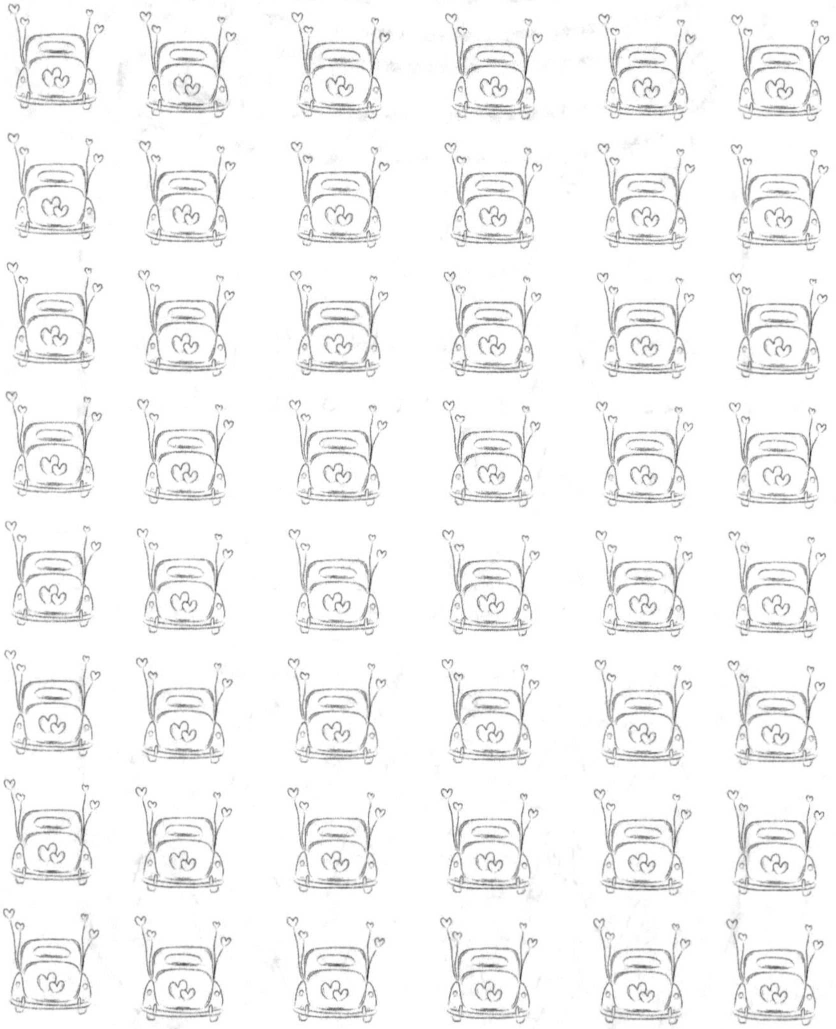

Wedding Fund

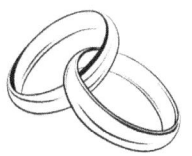

Goal _____

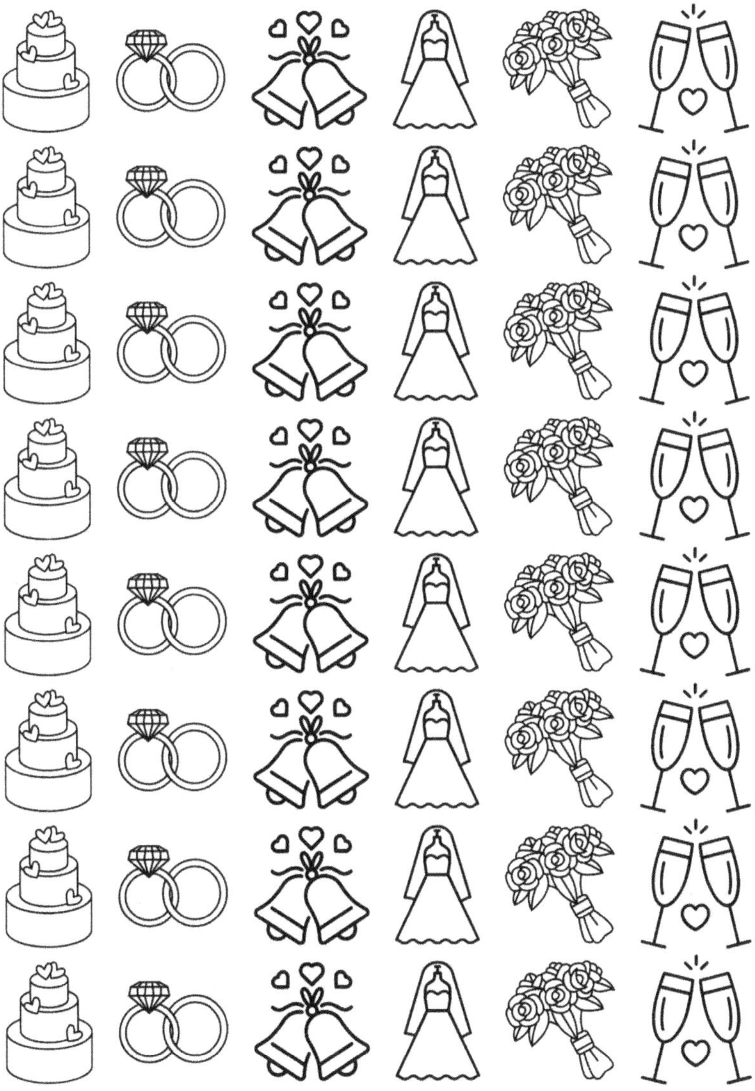

House Deposit Fund

Goal _____

House Deposit Fund

Goal _____

Home Refurbishment Fund

Goal _____

Home Refurbishment

Goal _____

Home Furnishings Fund

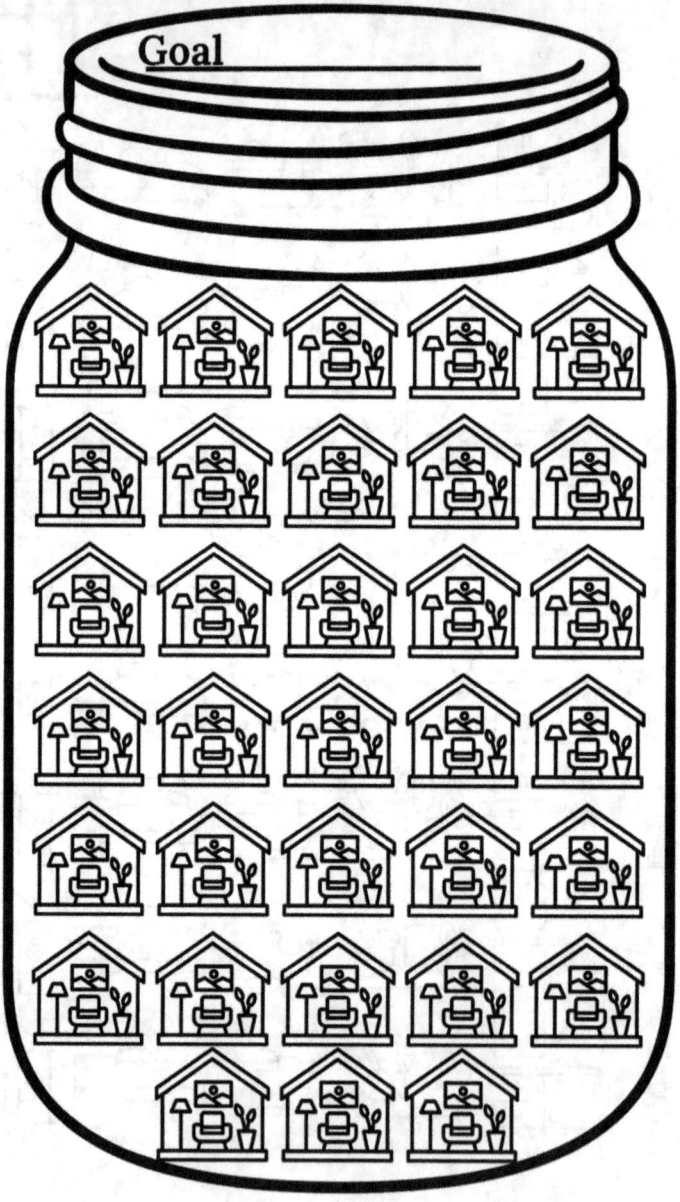

Goal _____

Home Furnishings

Goal _____

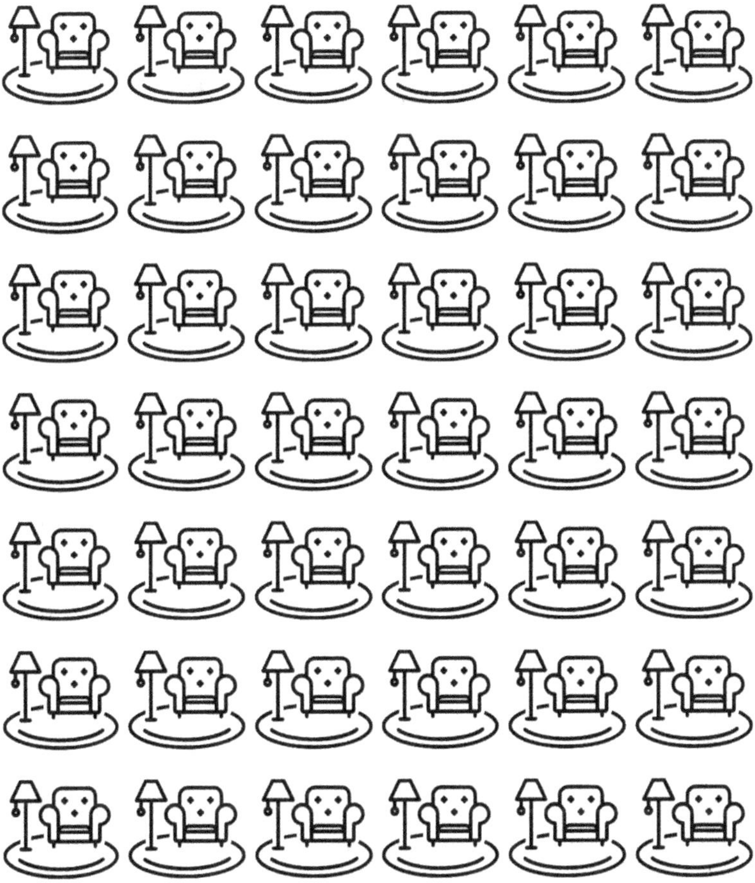

Home Decor Fund

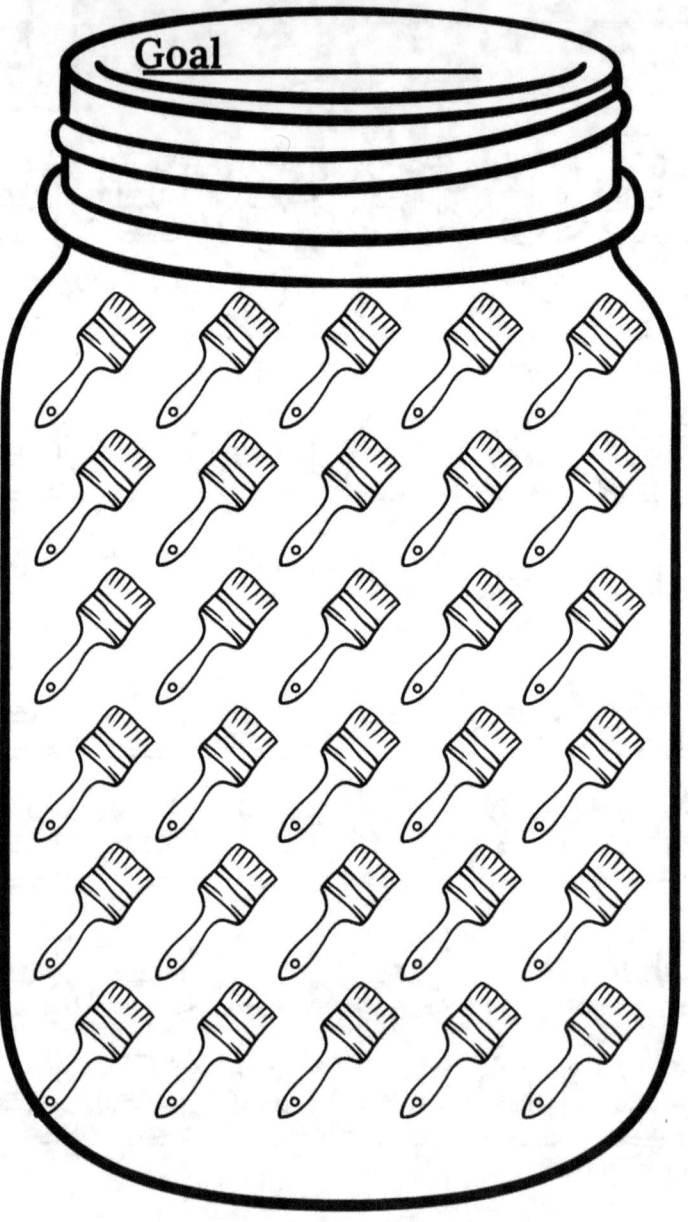

Goal _____

Home Decor

Goal _____

Home Decor

Goal _____

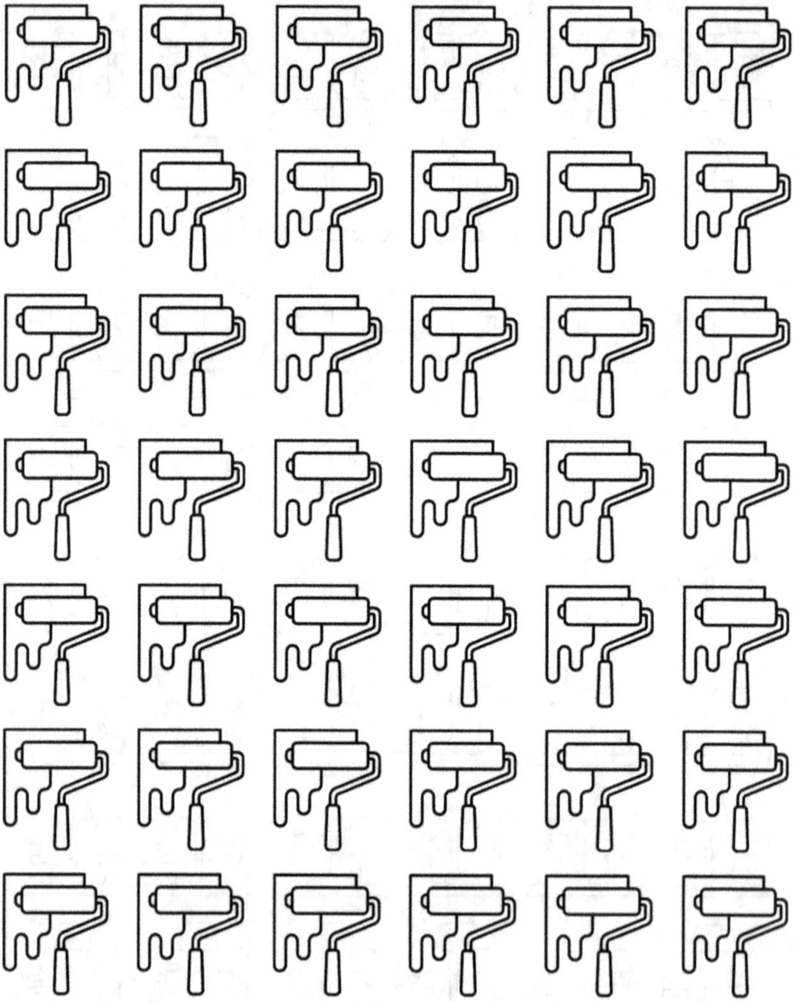

Car Savings Fund

Goal _____

New Car
<u>Goal</u>

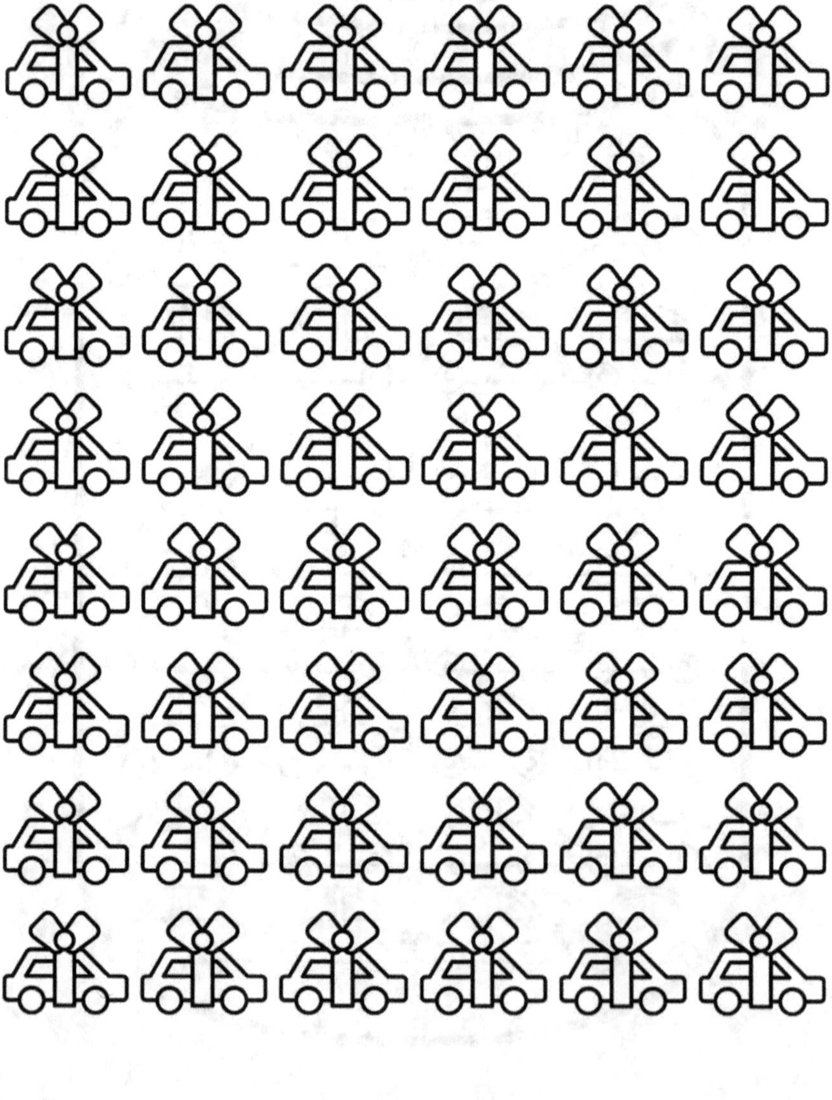

Car Repair Fund

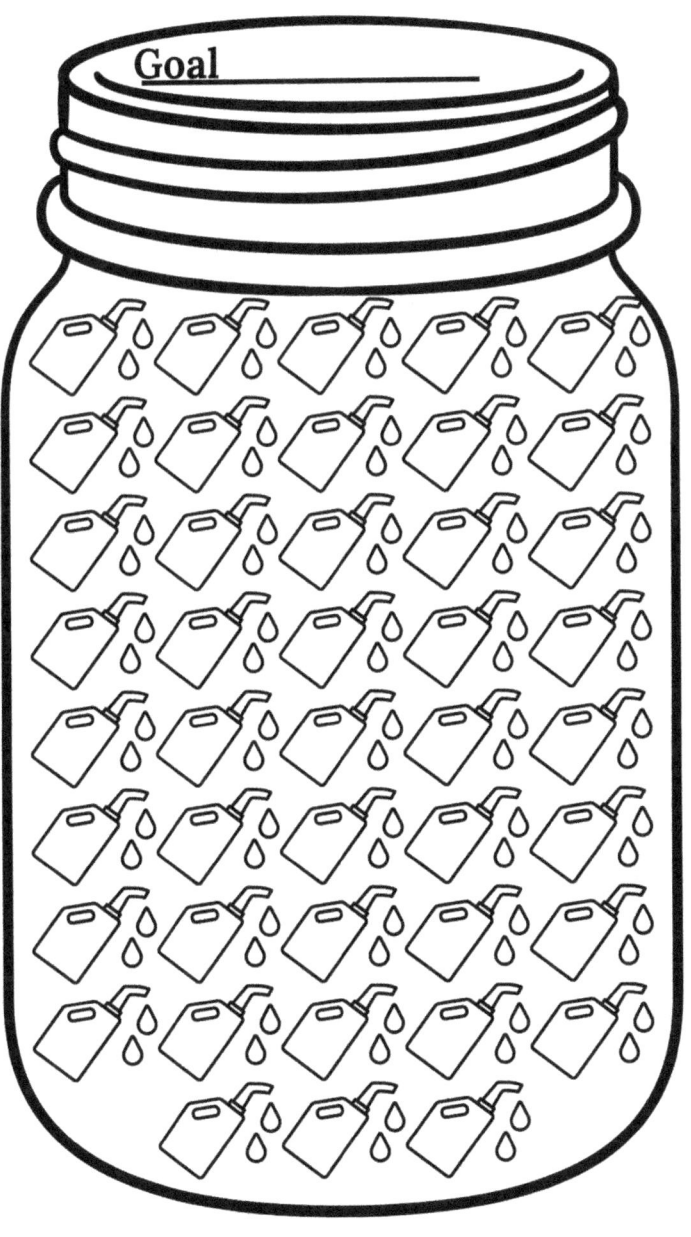

Goal _____

Car Repairs

Goal _____

Baby Savings Fund

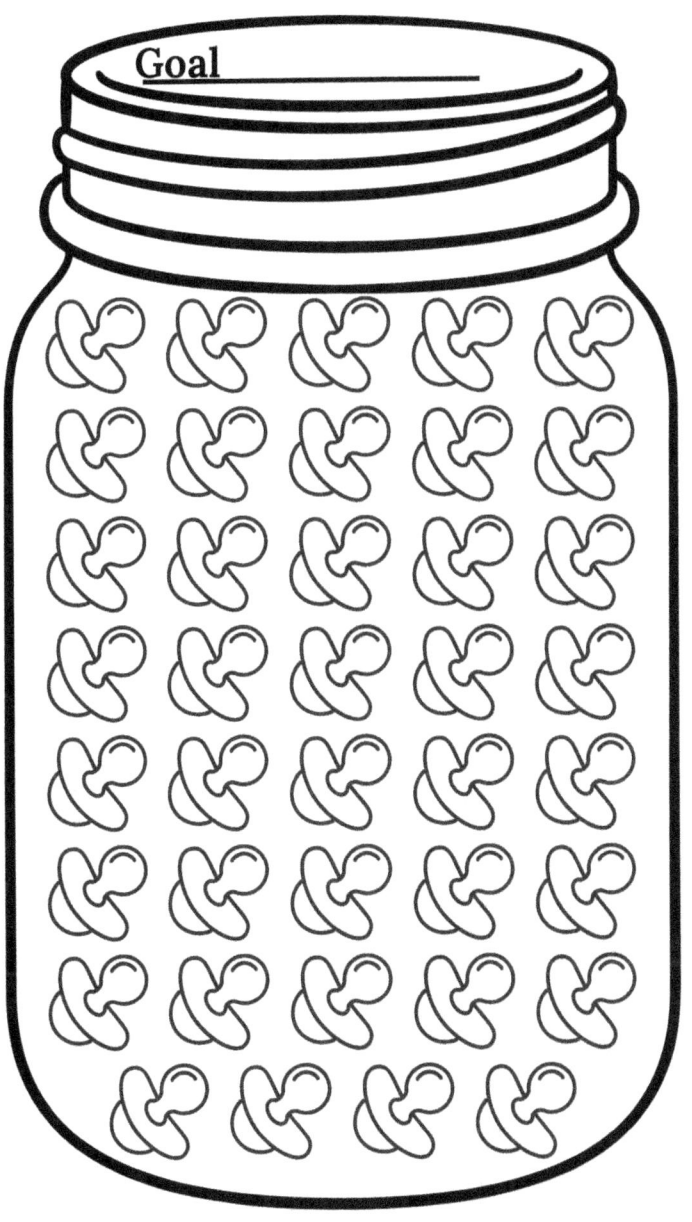

Goal _____

Baby Savings Fund

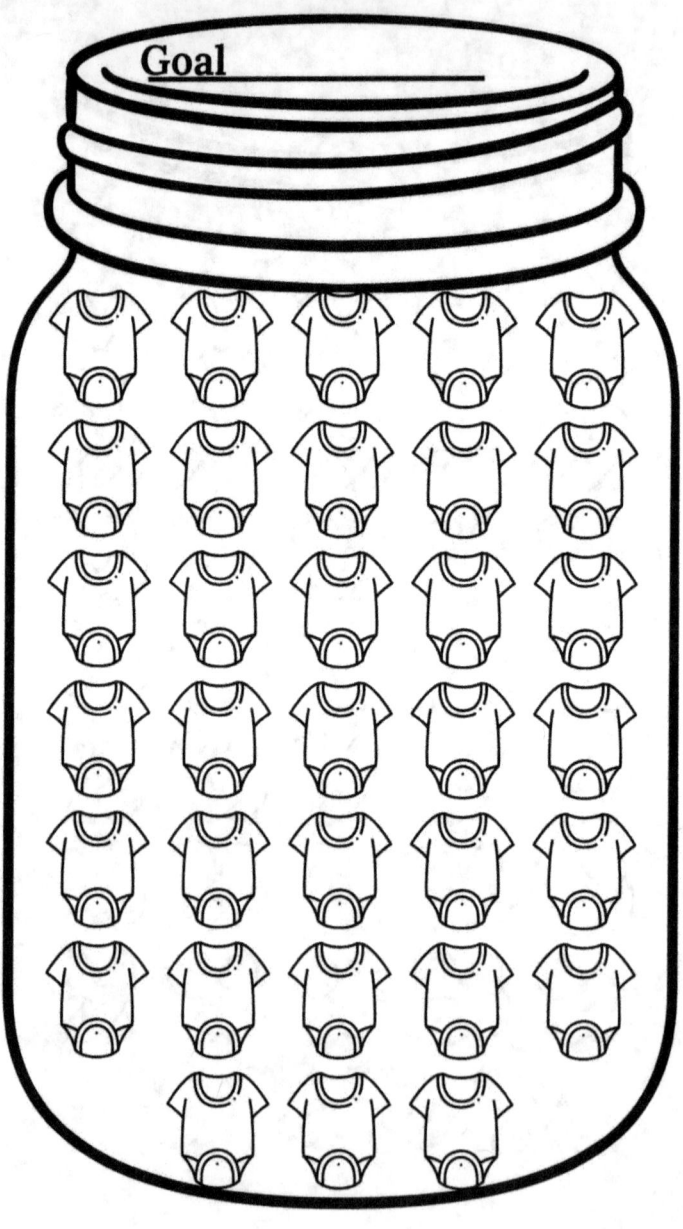

Goal _____

Baby Fund

Goal _____

Baby Fund

Goal _____

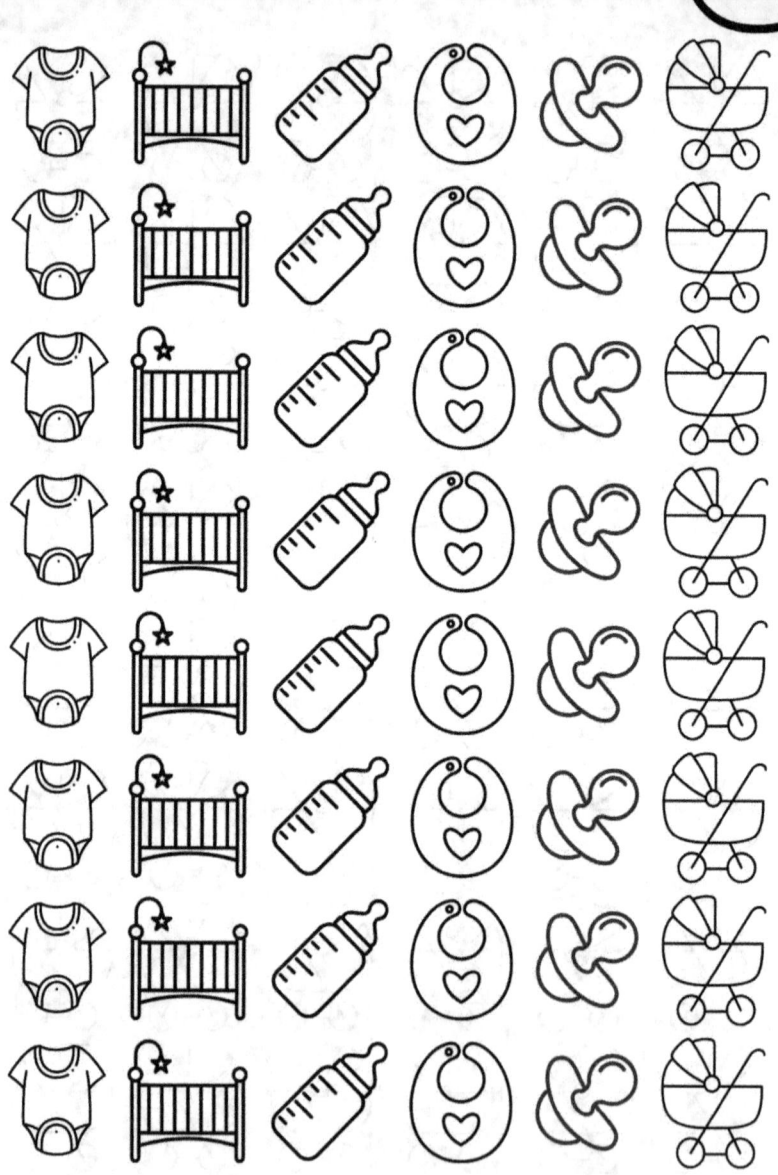

Pet Fund

Goal

Pet Fund

Goal _____

Clothing Fund

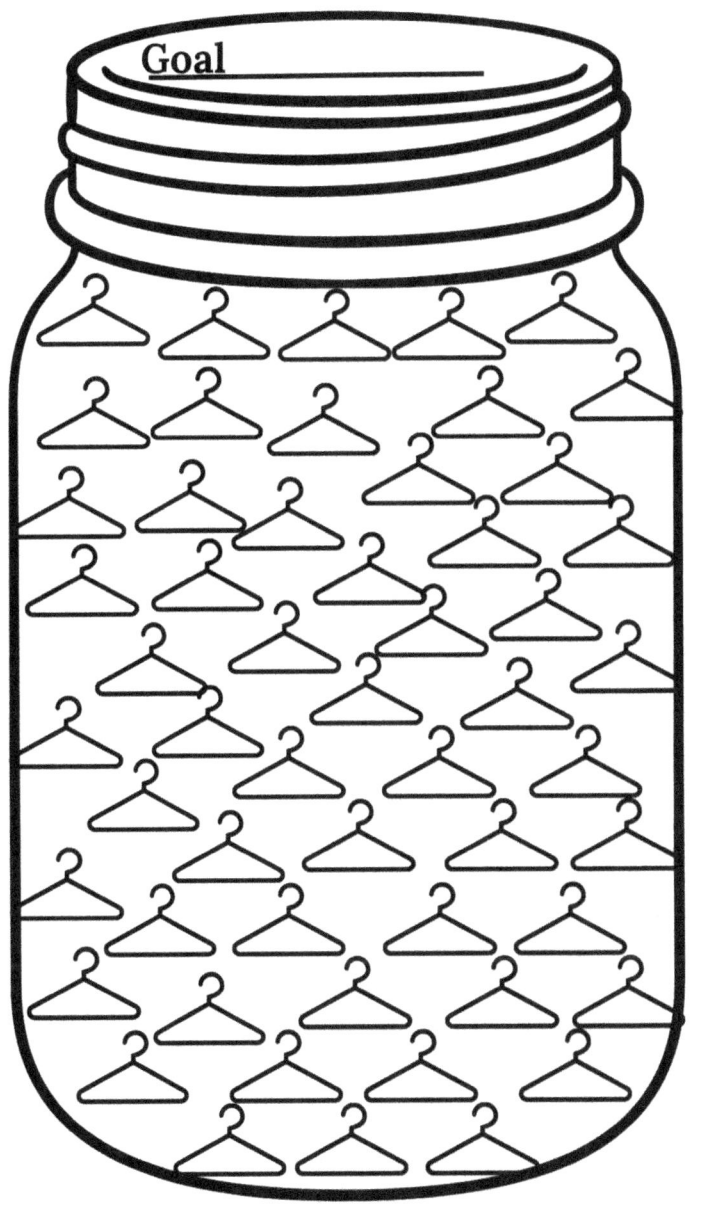

Goal _____

Clothing Fund

Goal _____

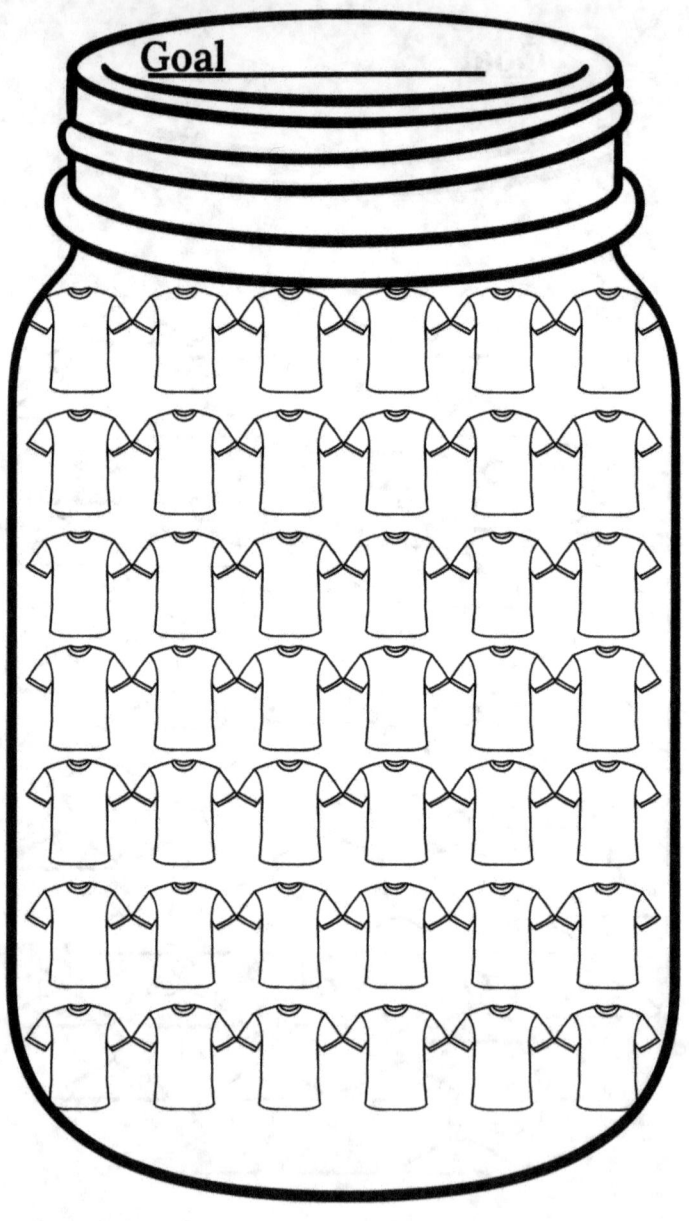

Shopping Spree Fund

Goal _____

Shopping Spree Fund
Goal _____

Self Care Fund

Goal _____

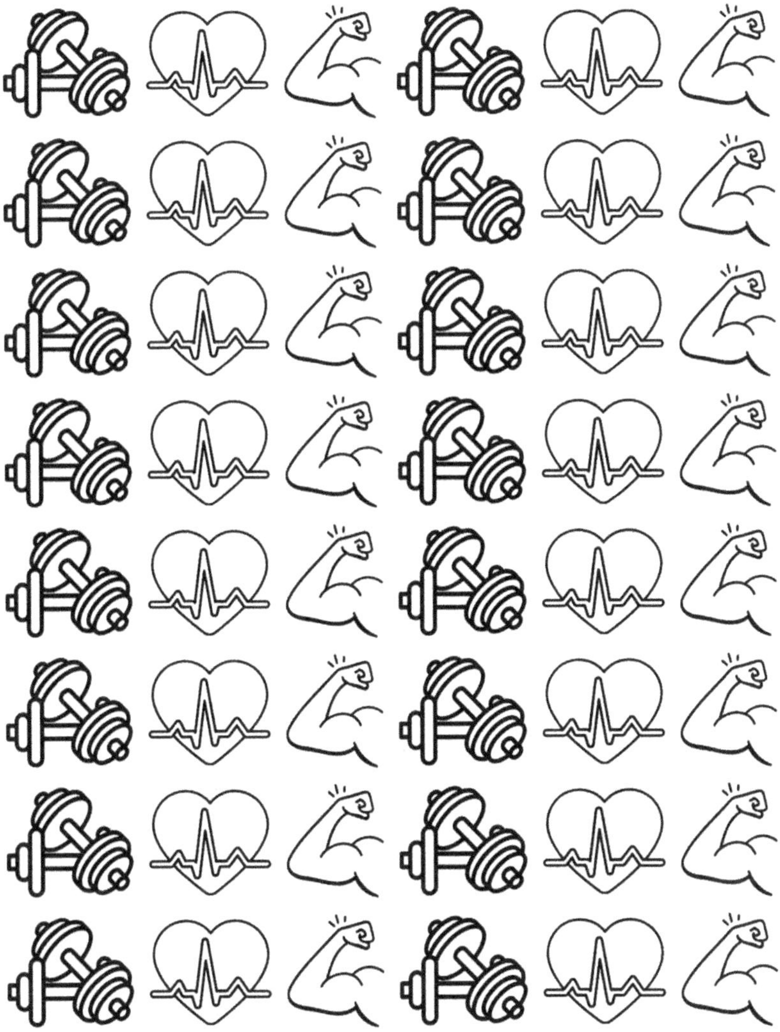

Self Care Fund

Goal _____

Health Care Fund

Goal _____

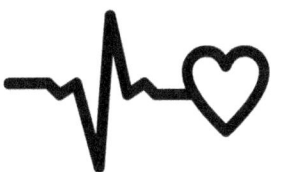

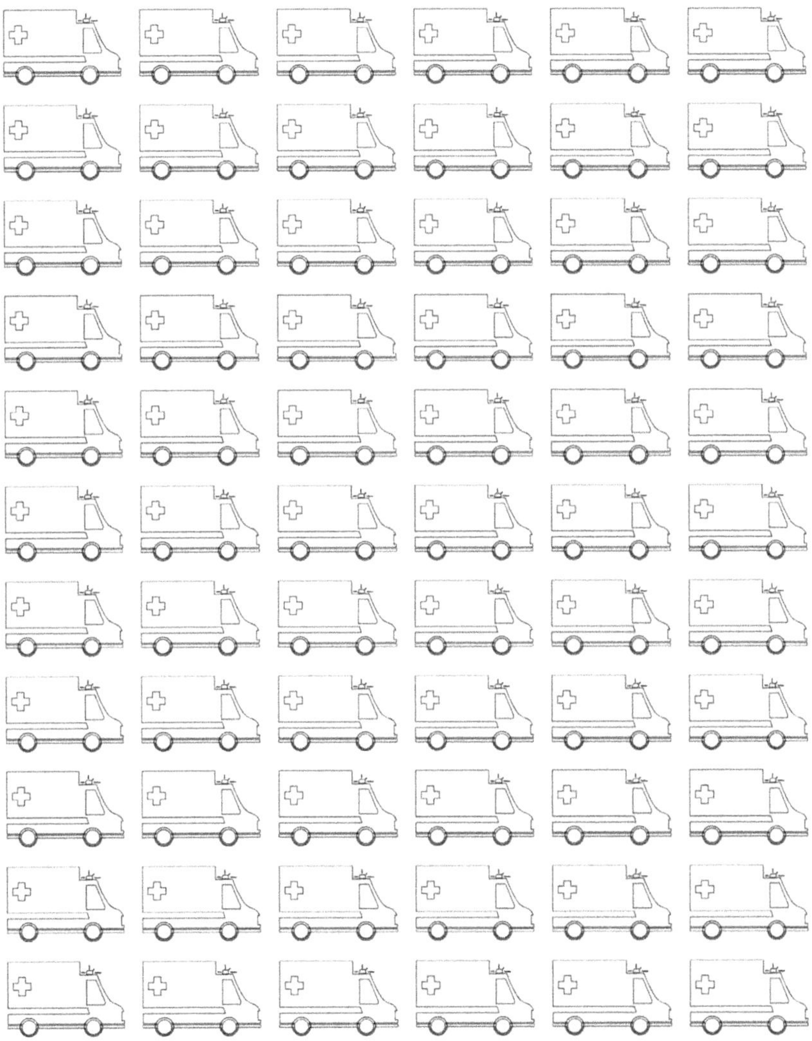

Health Care Fund

Goal
_____

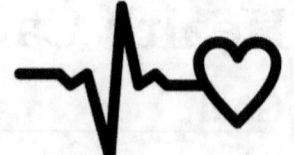

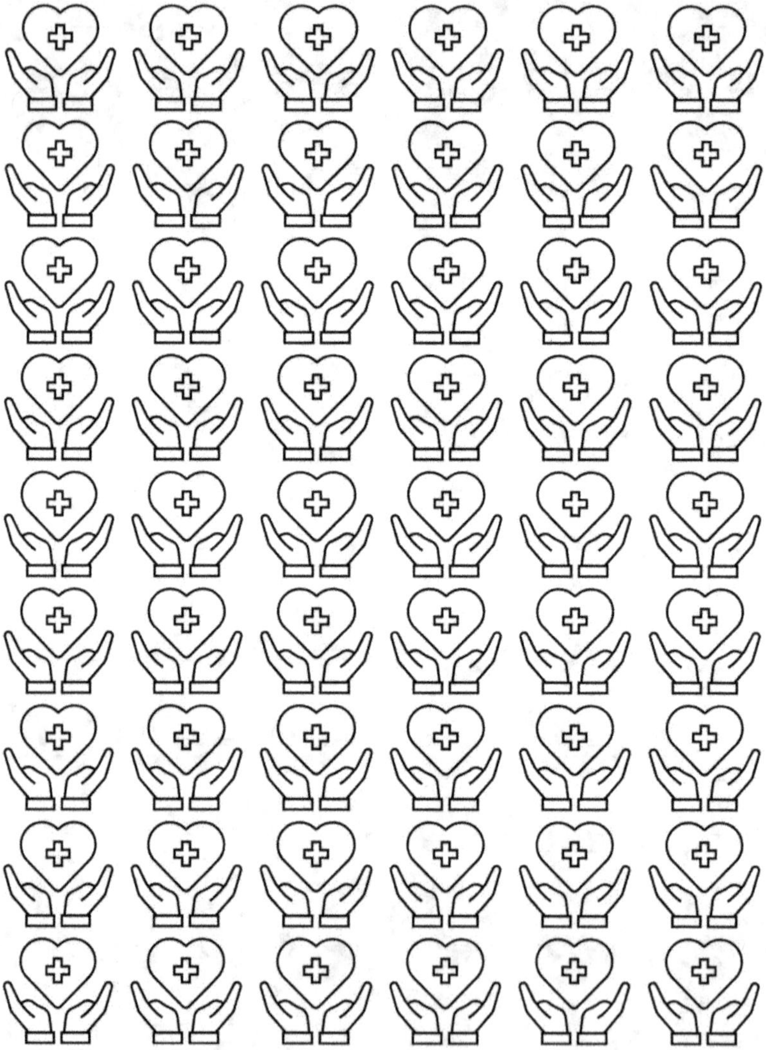

Health Care Fund

Goal _____

Save for.....
General Savings

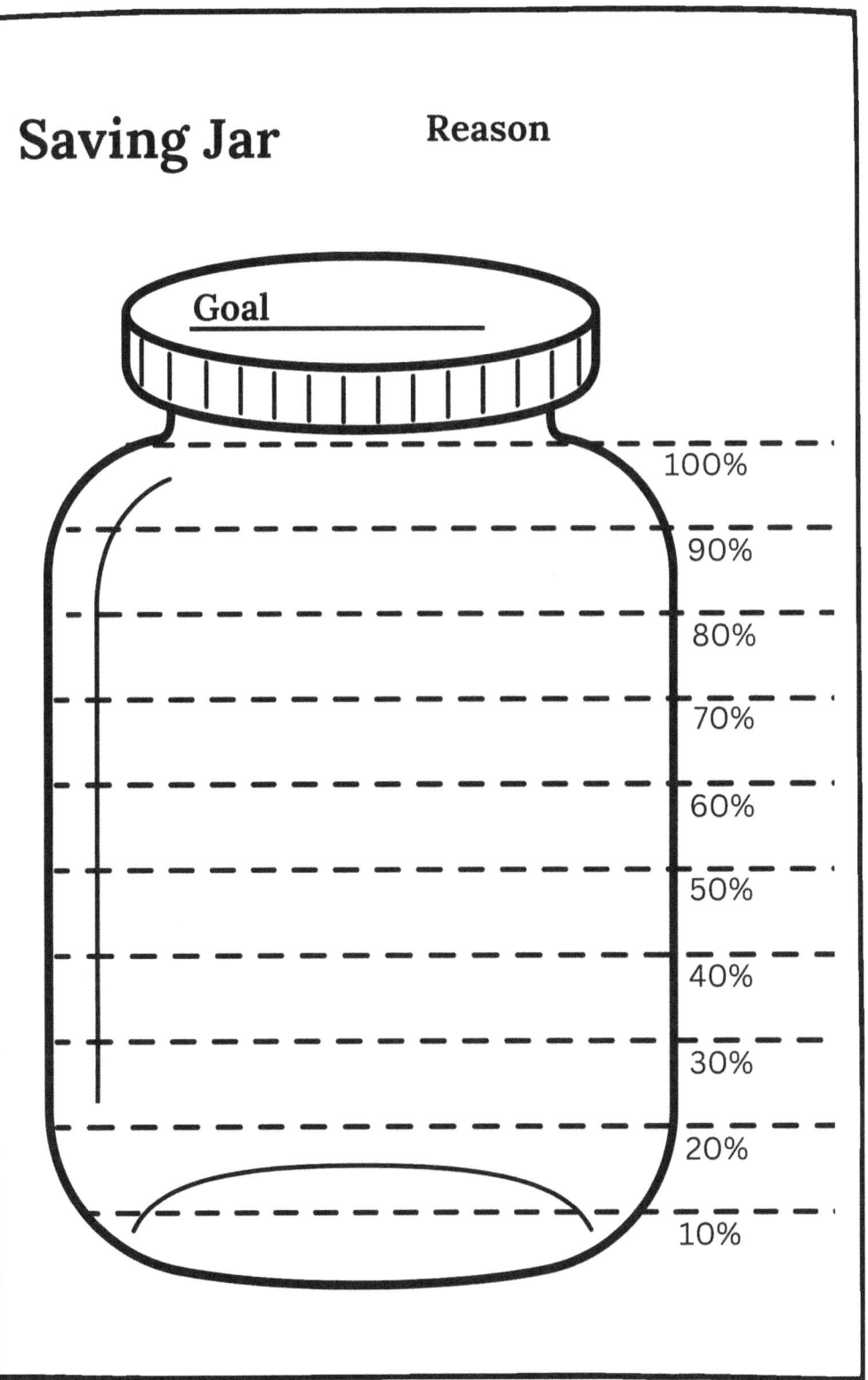

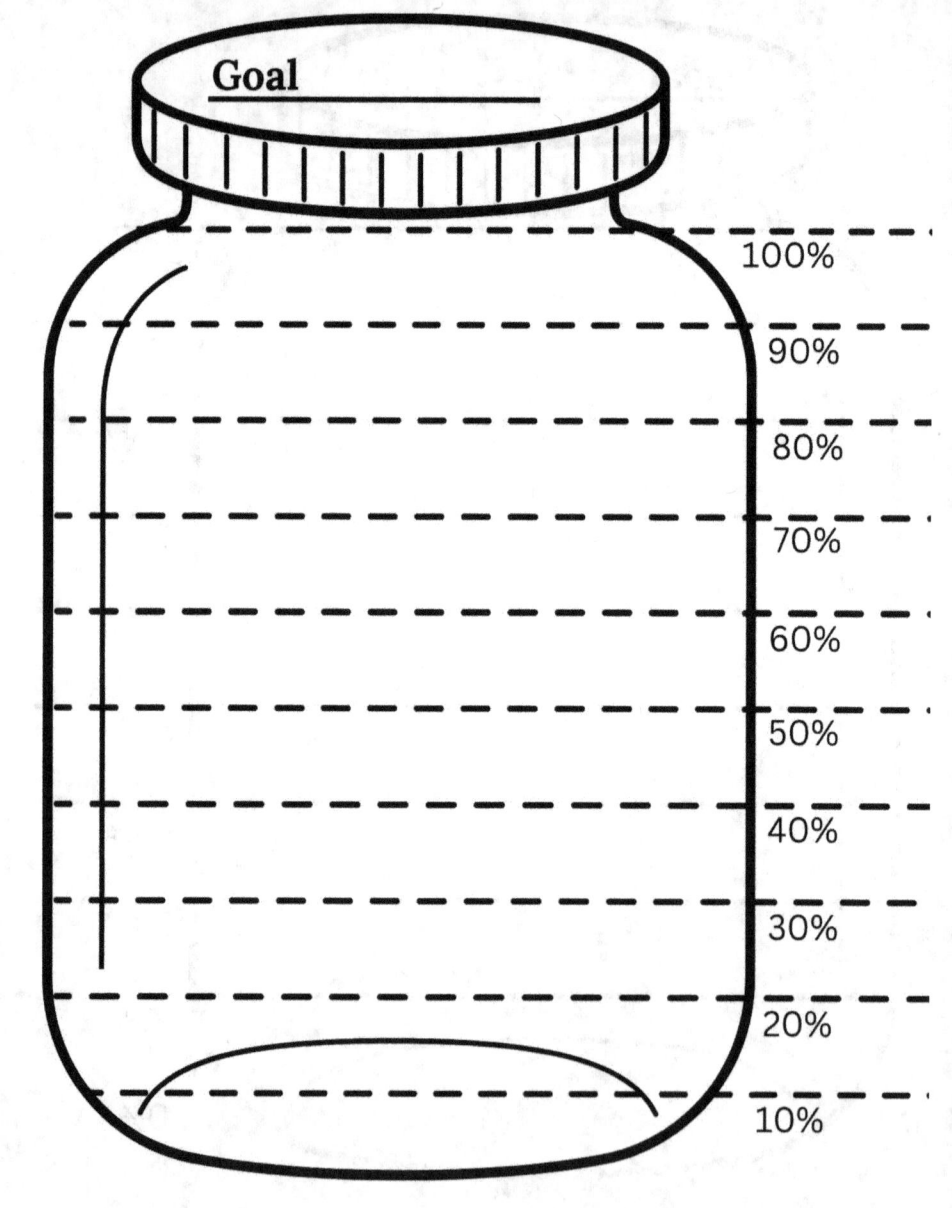

Saving Jar

Reason

Goal

- 100%
- 90%
- 80%
- 70%
- 60%
- 50%
- 40%
- 30%
- 20%
- 10%

Saving Jar

Reason

Goal

- 100%
- 90%
- 80%
- 70%
- 60%
- 50%
- 40%
- 30%
- 20%
- 10%

Saving Jar

Goal _____

Saving Jar

Goal _____

Saving Jar

Saving Jar

Goal _____

Saving Jar

Saving Jar

Saving Jar

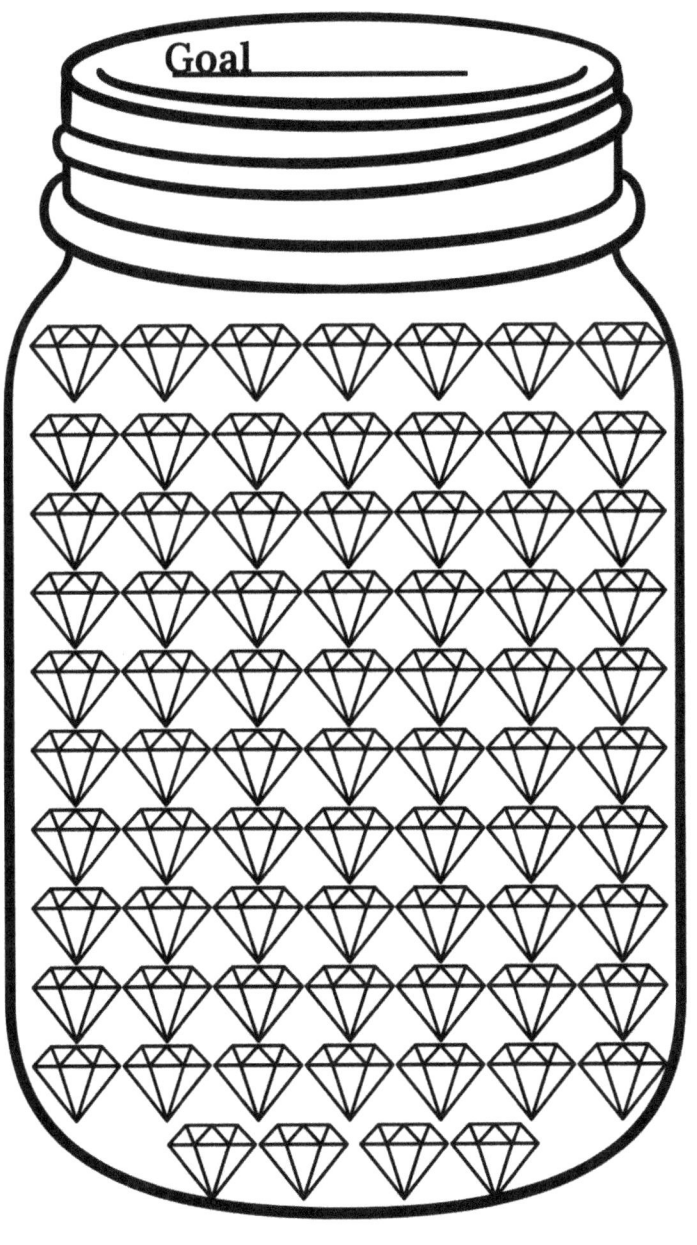

Saving Jar

Saving Jar

Saving Jar

Goal _____

Saving Jar

Saving Jar

Goal _____

Saving Jar

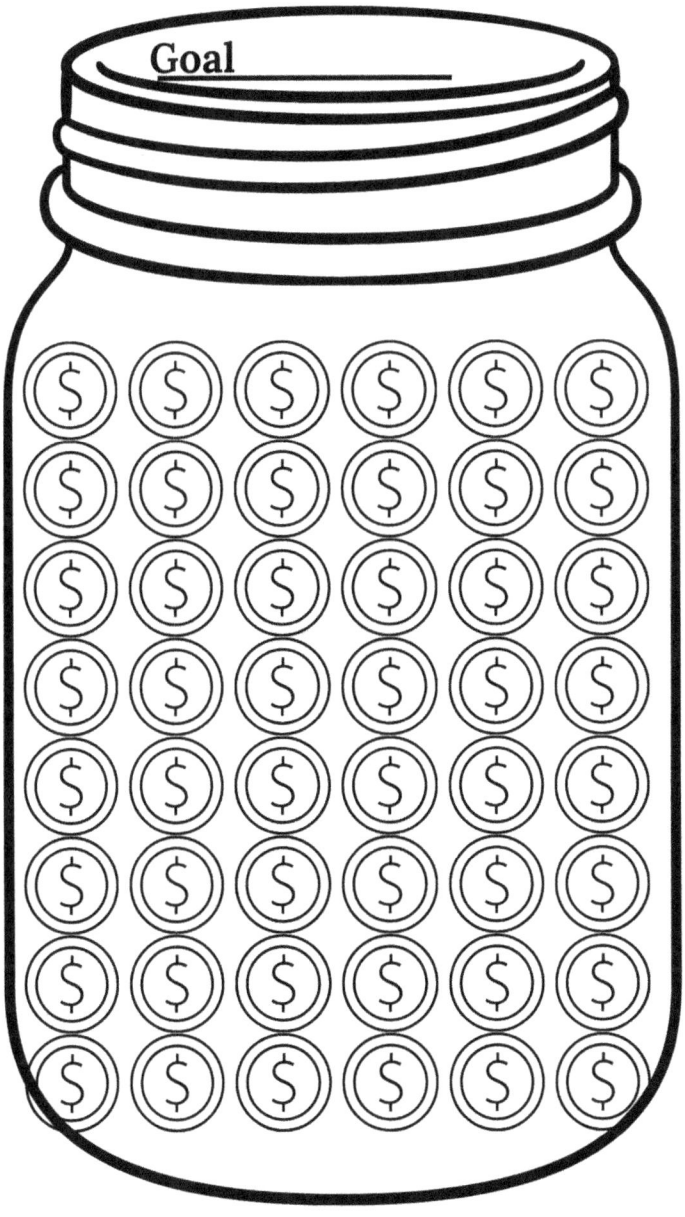

Saving Jar

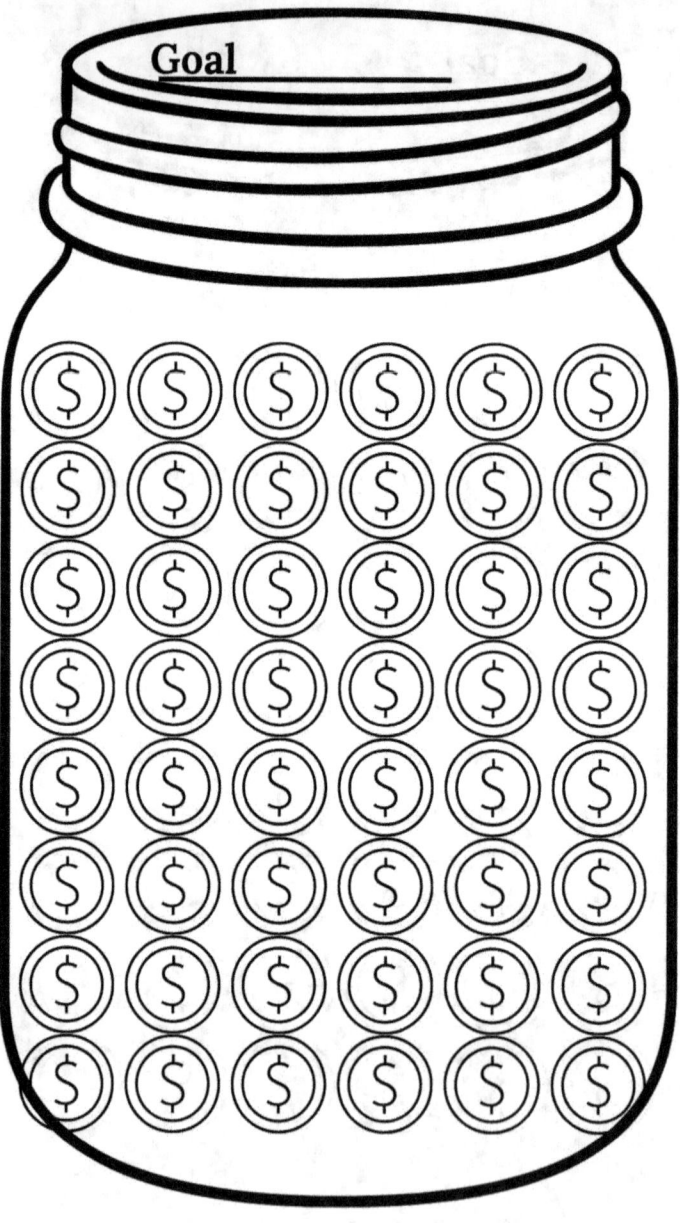

Saving Jar

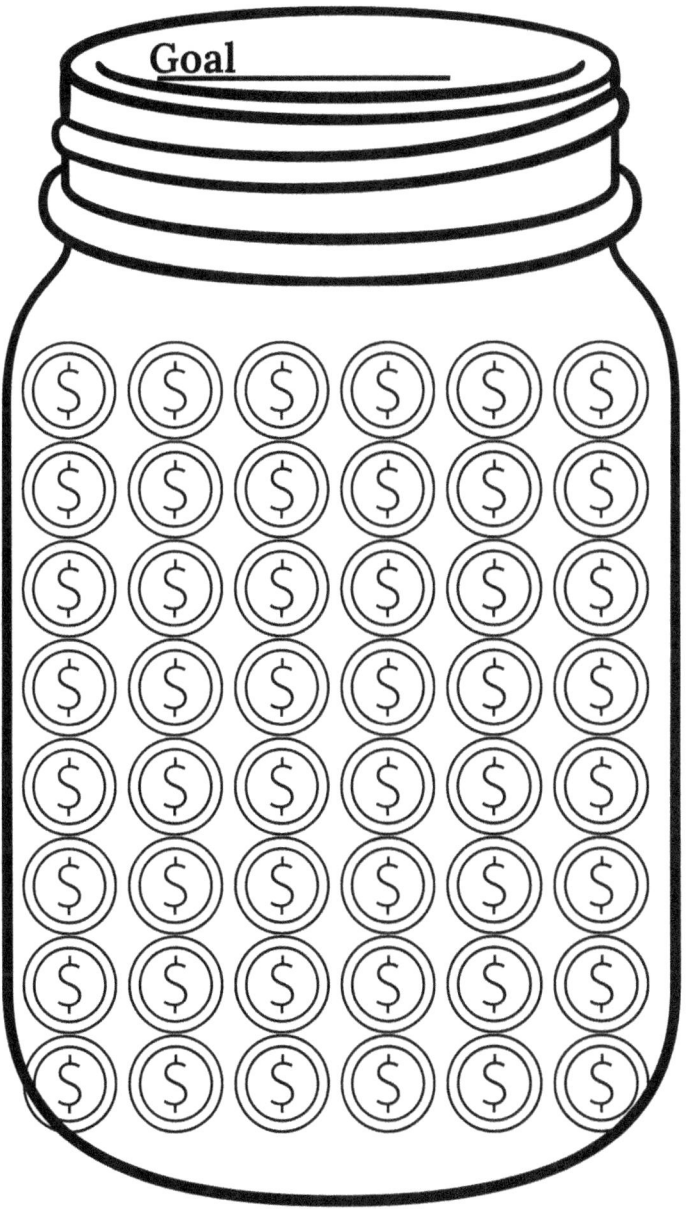

Saving Jar

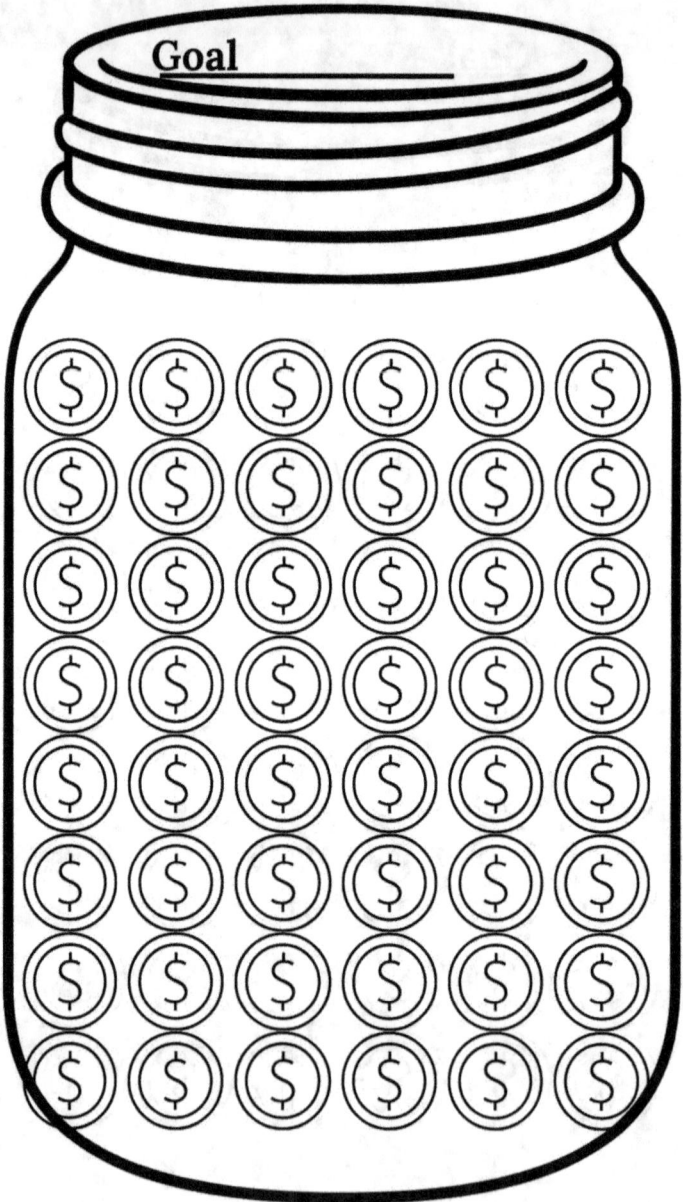

Goal _____

Save for.....
Debt Repayment

Debt Payment

Paid _____

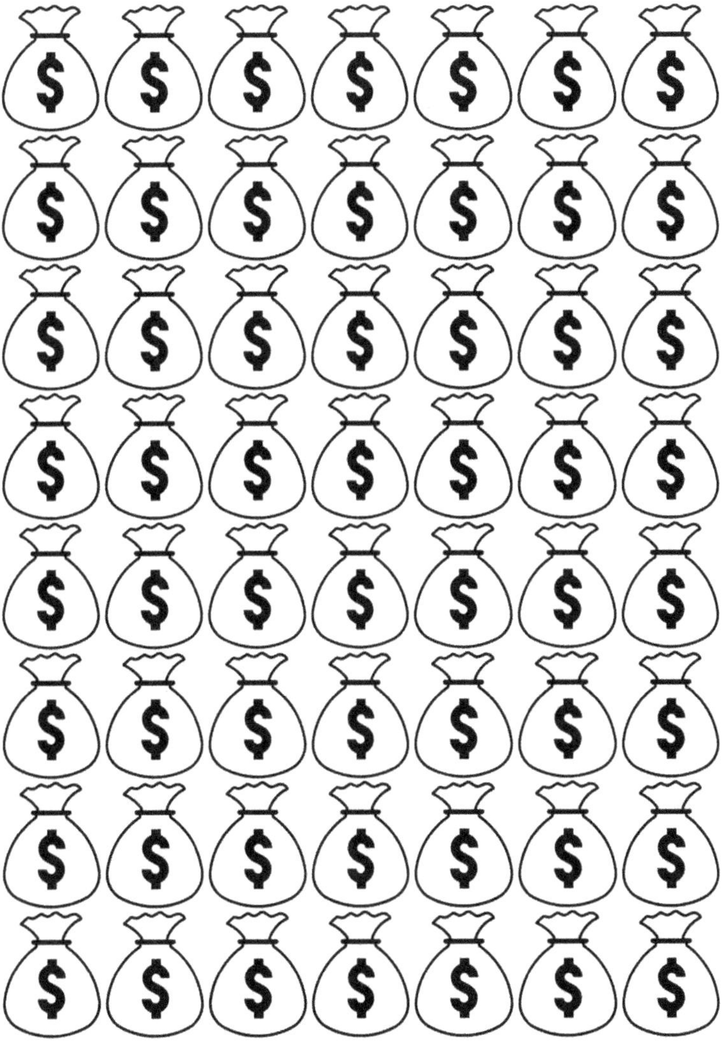

Debt Payment

Paid _____

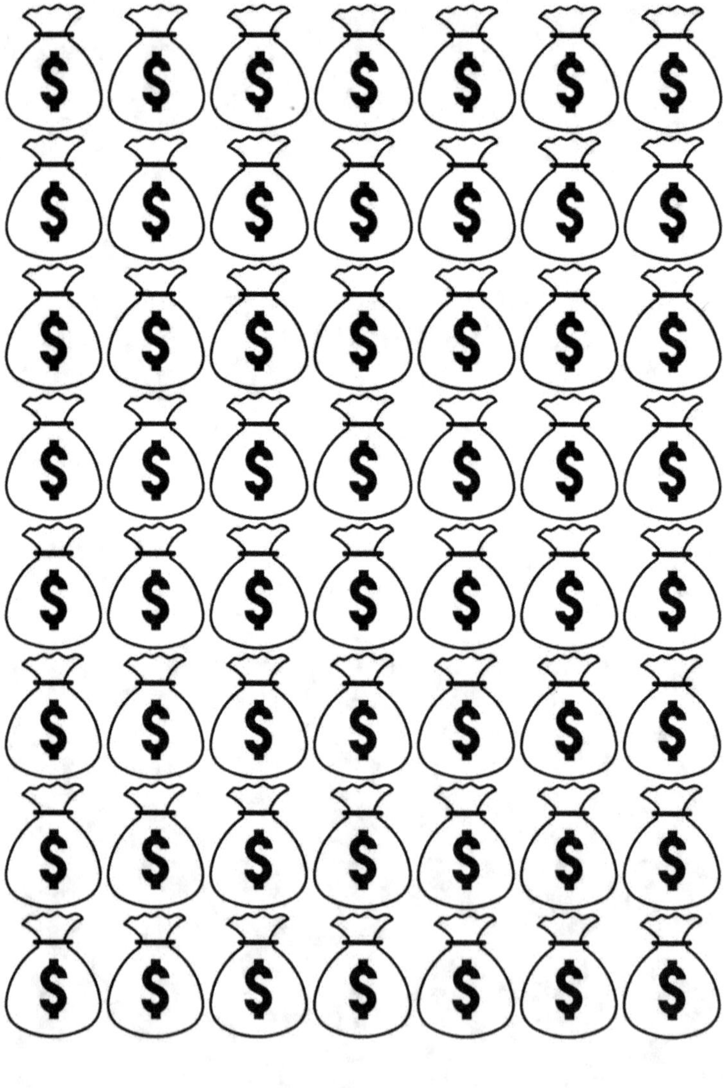

Debt Payment

Paid _____

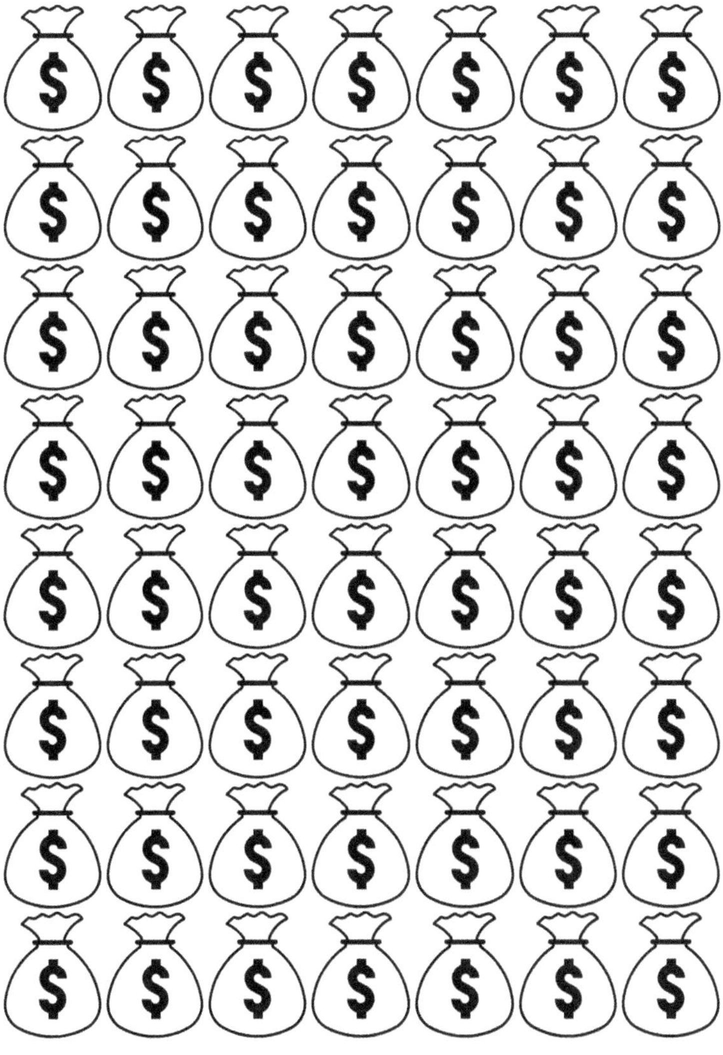

Debt Payment

Paid _____

Credit Card Payment

Paid _____

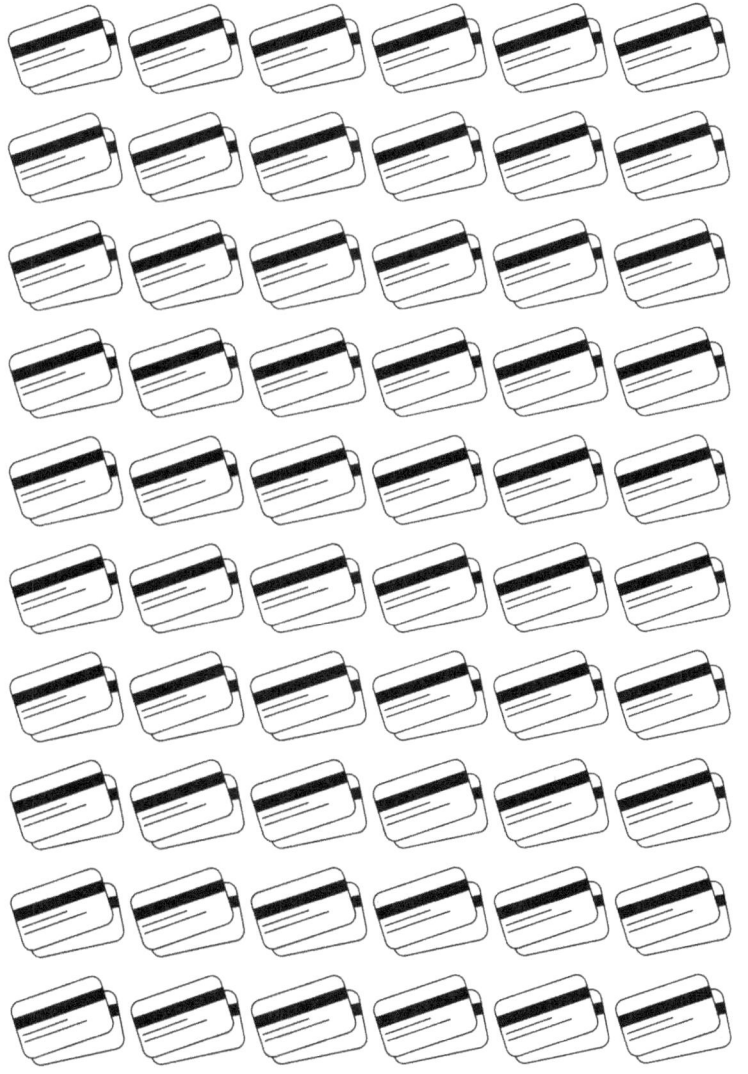

Credit Card Payment

Paid _____

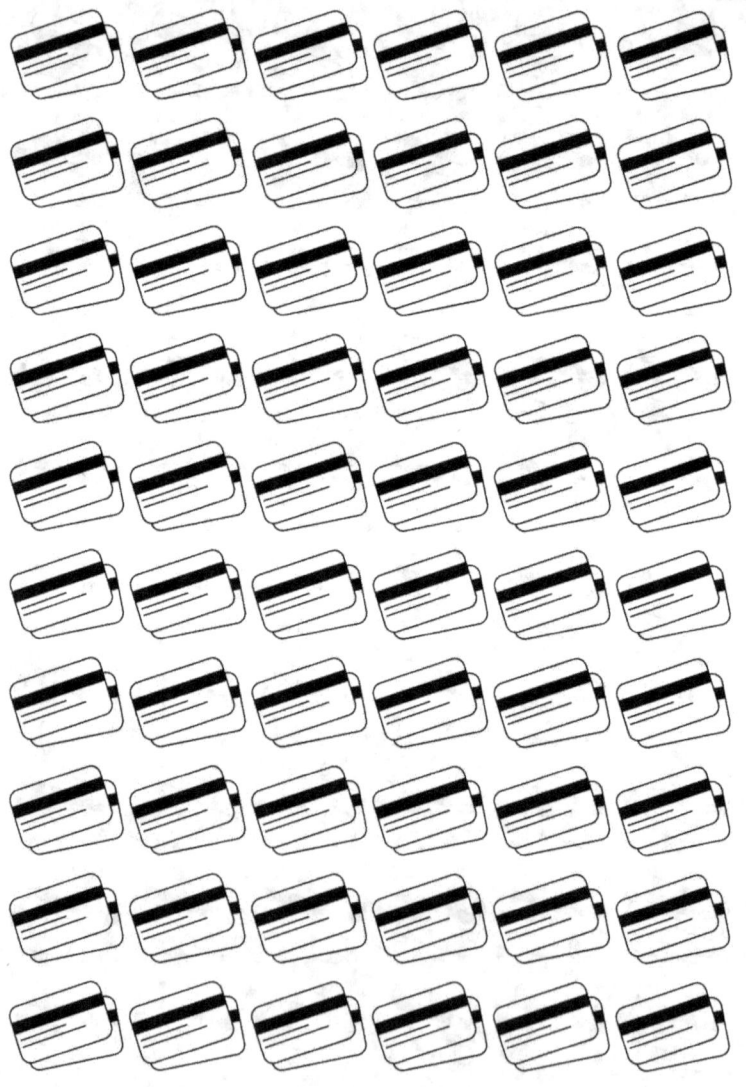

Credit Card Payment

Paid _____

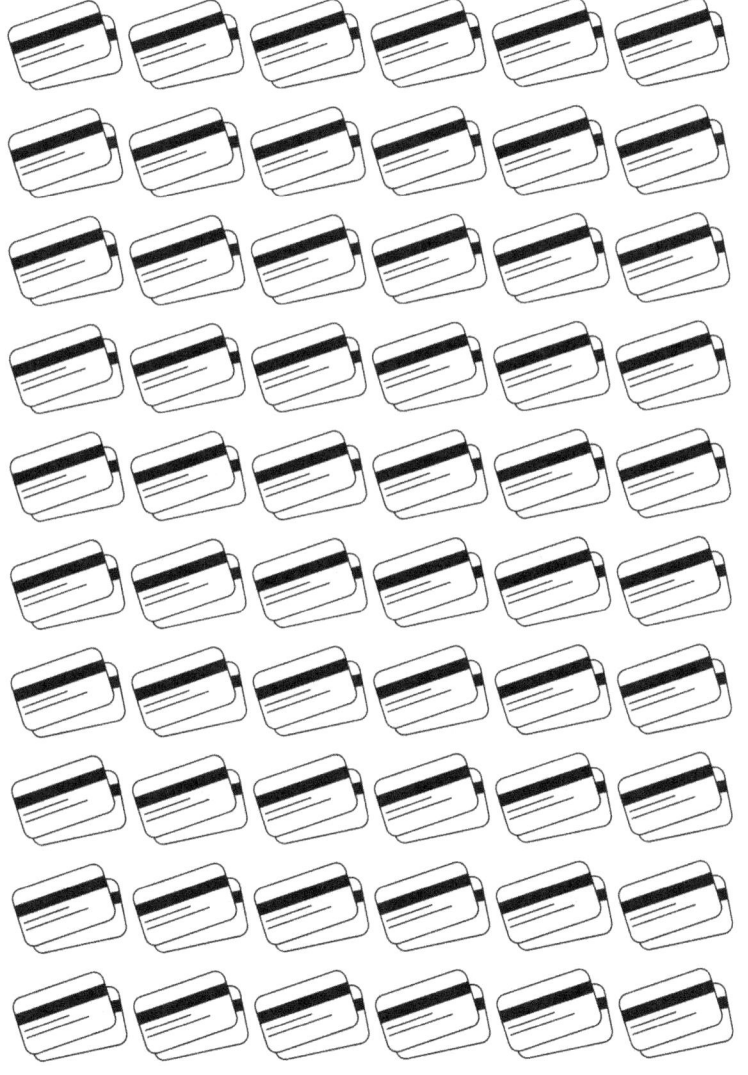

Credit Card Payment

Paid _____

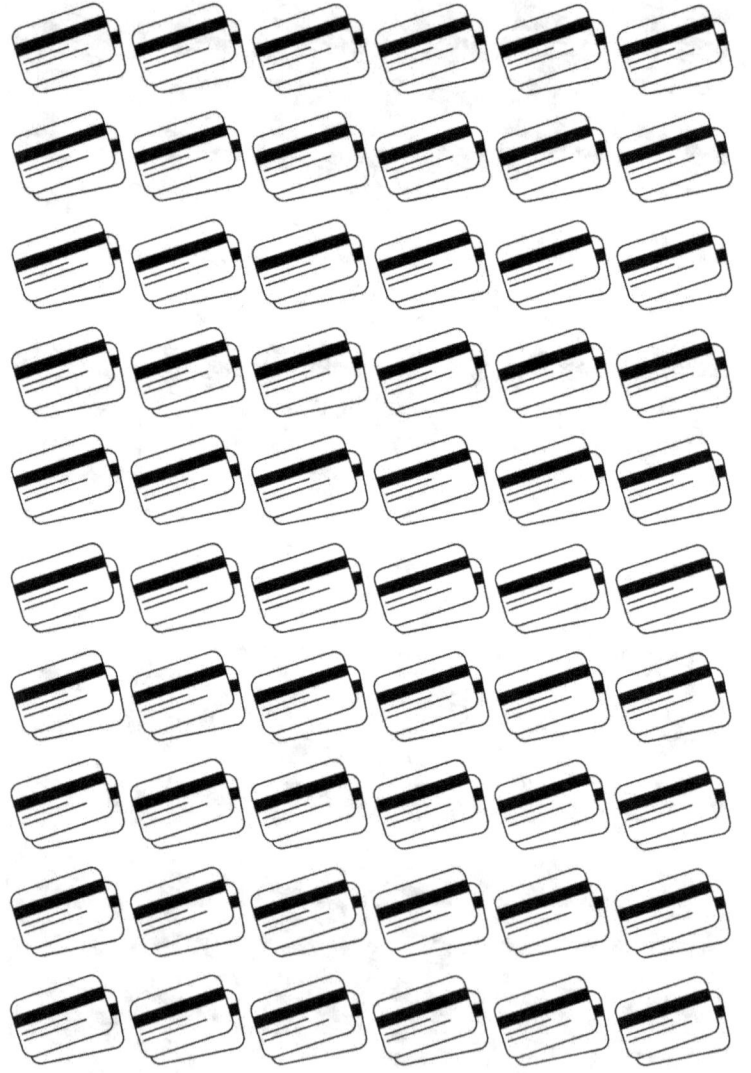

Save for.....
Christmas

Christmas Fund

Christmas Fund

Goal _____

Christmas Fund

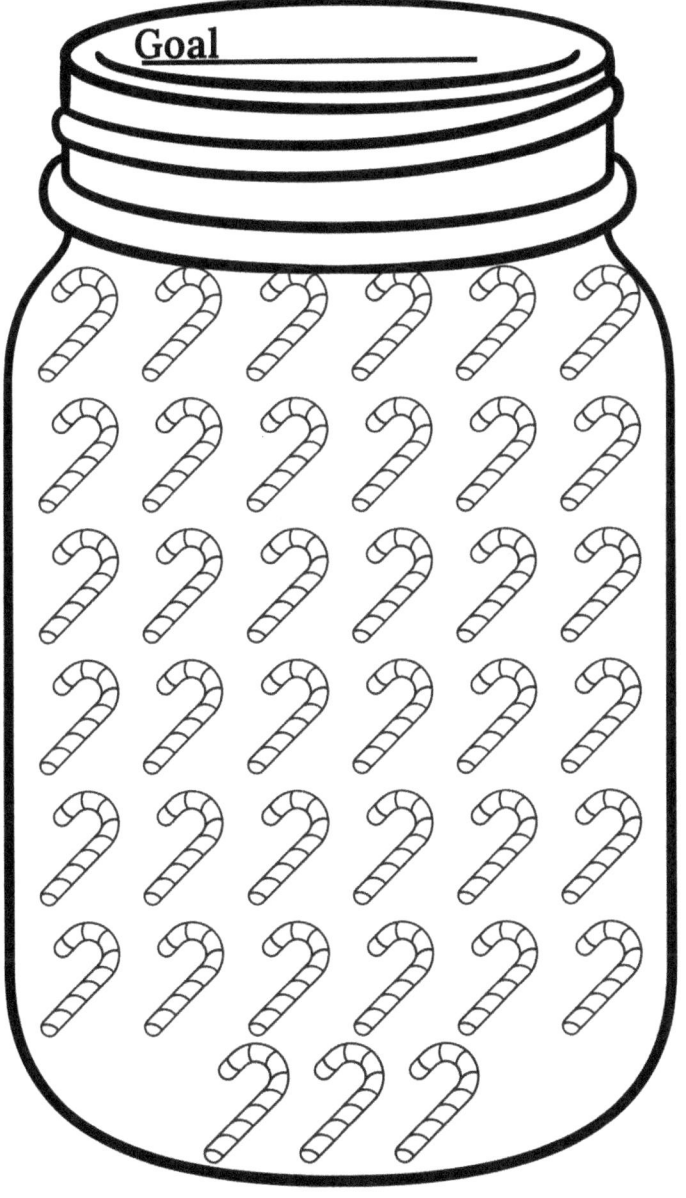

Goal _____

Christmas Fund

Goal _____

Christmas Fund

Christmas Fund

Goal _____

Christmas Fund

Goal _____

www.ingramcontent.com/pod-product-compliance
Lightning Source LLC
Chambersburg PA
CBHW052321220526
45472CB00001B/214